Dedication.

THIS BOOK HAS DEEN PREPARED FOR THE BENEFIT OF THOSE WHO PATRONIZE THE BEST BAR-ROOMS. WINE-ROOMS, AND CLUB-ROOMS, SO THAT THEY MAY KNOW WHAT IS REALLY GOOD, AND WHEN AND WHERE THEY CAN GET IT. IF THAT CLASS SHALL BE BENEFITED, THEN THE WRITER WILL FEEL AMPLY REPAID FOR THE TIME AND TROUBLE HE HAS EXPENDED, AND WILL FEEL THAT A LIFE SPENT IN THE SERVICE OF GOOD TASTE HAS NOT BEEN IN VAIN.

First published by
Lawlor & Co., Cincinnati.
1895

This edition is published
by Wichne Bok
www.wichnebok.no
2021

THE MIXICOLOGIST

OR

HOW TO MIX ALL KINDS

OF FANCY DRINKS

CONTAINING CLEAR AND RELIABLE DIRECTIONS FOR MIXING ALL THE DIFFERENT BEVERAGES USED IN THE UNITED STATES, EMBRACING JULEPS, COBBLERS, COCKTAILS, PUNCHES, DURKEES, "TRILBYS," ETC.,

ETC., IN ENDLESS VARIETY, WITH SOME RECIPES ON COOKING, AND OTHER GENERAL INFORMATION

AN UP-TO-DATE RECIPE BOOK

BY C. F. LAWLOR

RECENTLY

CHIEF BARTENDER OF THE

GRAND HOTEL

AND NOW AT

BURNET HOUSE, CINCINNATI.

FOR SALE BY

THE ROBERT CLARKE COMPANY

HAWLEY'S

AND UNION NEWS COMPANY

INTRODUCTORY.

THIS is an age of progress. New ideas and new appliances follow each other in rapid succession to meet the ever-increasing demand for novelties, which adiminister to creature comforts and gratification to fastidious tastes. "The Mixicologist" is intended to meet this demand.

It is with feelings of modesty and diffidence that I approach so important a subject, but my long experience, and my hearty desire to produce what I hope will become a standard, and thus to help my fellow workers, and also to elevate the tone of our profession, prompts the undertaking.

These, I trust, are sufficient reasons for my attempting to write the following. If to "tend bar" consisted only in filling up glasses thoughtlessly, and pushing them out to customers carelessly, it would not be proper to speak of it as a polite vocation and a fine art, and it would be useless to write on the subject. But I place it among the more elegant employments of life, and to be a successful bartender requires the exercise of those finer faculties that distinguish the cultured artist from the inexperienced, and which are so much appreciated by gentlemen customers.

Also, in this introductory, I feel it my duty to thank my friends for information received for this little book, among them being Mr. John H. Kuhn, steward of the Grand Hotel; Col. Billy Clarke, and Mr. James McGlade, Weddell House, Cleveland, Ohio, hoping it will be found useful, not only to the saloon, but to others. Recipes, etc., will be readily found by index.

Respectfully,

THE AUTHOR.

INDEX.

INTRODUCTORY	9
STOCK FOR A FIRST-CLASS BAR.	19
HOW TO MIX ALL DRINKS.	21
"'Arf and 'Arf."	21
A Reviver.	21
Absinthe Cocktail.	21
Absinthe Frappe.	21
Ale Sangaree.	21
An Eye-opener.	22
Apple Brandy Cocktail.	22
Apple Toddy.	22
Attorney General.	22
B. & S.	22
Beef Tea.	22
Benedictine.	23
Big 4 Mint Julep.	23
Bijou Cocktail.	23
Bishop.	23
Bowl of Claret Punch.	25
Brandy and Ginger Ale.	25
Brandy and Gum.	25
Brandy and Mint.	25
Brandy and Rum Punch.	25
Brandy and Soda.	26
Brandy Cocktail.	26
Brandy Crust.	26
Brandy Daisy.	27
Brandy Fix.	27
Brandy Fizz.	27
Brandy Flip.	27

Brandy Julep.	28
Brandy Punch.	28
Brandy Sangaree.	28
Brandy Smash.	28
Brandy Sour.	29
Brandy Sour.	29
Brandy Toddy.	29
Buffalo.	29
Burnt Brandy.	29
Catawba Cobbler.	30
Champagne Cobbler.	30
Champagne Cocktail — (Plain.)	30
Champagne Cup.	30
Champagne Julep.	30
Champagne Punch.	31
Chocolate Cocktail.	31
Claret Cobbler.	31
Claret Cup.	31
Claret Flip.	32
Claret Punch.	32
Coffee Cobbler.	32
Coffee Cocktail.	32
Creme de Menthe.	33
Curaçoa Punch.	33
Dripped Absinthe.	33
Duke of Norfolk Punch.	33
Durkee.	34
Dutch Cocktail.	34
Egg Sour.	34
Eggnog in Quantity.	34
Eggnog.	35

English Bishop. 35

Gin Crust. 35

Gin Daisy. 35

Gin Fizz. 36

Gin Julep. 36

Gin Sangaree. 36

Gin Smash. 36

Golden Fizz. 36

Golden Slipper. 37

Half and Half. 37

Half and Half. (Dublin Style.) 37

Hendrick Cocktail. 37

High Ball. 37

Hints on Using Ice. 37

Hock Cobbler. 38

Hot Brandy. 38

Hot Eggnog. 38

Hot English Ale Flip. 38

Hot English Rum Flip. 38

Hot Irish Whiskey Punch. 39

Hot Milk Punch. 39

Hot Scotch Whiskey Punch. 39

Hot Spiced Rum. 39

Hot Rum. 40

Hot Whiskey Sling. 40

How to Serve Tom and Jerry. 40

Improved Brandy Cocktail. 40

Improved Tom Gin Cocktail. 41

Improved Whiskey Cocktail. 41

Irish Cocktail. 41

John Collins. 41

K and K Punch. 41

Kentucky Toddy. 42

La Casino Fizz. 42

Lawlor's Pousse Cafe. 42

Lemonade. 42

Manhattan Cocktail. 42

Manhattan Milk Punch. 43

Martinez Cocktail. 43

Milk Punch. 43

Milk Punch. 43

Morning Cocktail. 44

Old-fashioned Cocktail. 44

Old-fashioned Punch. 44

Old-fashioned Toddy. 44

Parisian Pousse Cafe. 44

Pineapple Julep. 45

Plain Lemonade. 45

Pony Brandy. 45

Port Wine Flip. 45

Port Wine Sangaree. 46

Porter Cup. 46

Porter Sangaree. 46

Pousse l'Amour. 46

Punch a la Dwyer. 47

Punch a la Romaine. 47

Remsen Cooler. 48

Rhine Wine and Seltzer. 48

Rhine Wine Cobbler. 48

Rickey. 48

Rock and Rye. 48

Roman Punch. 48

Rum Sour. 49

Sauterne Cobbler. 49

Shandy Gaff. 49

Sheridan Punch or Float. 49

Sherry and Bitters. 49

Sherry and Egg. 49

Sherry and Ice. 50

Sherry Cobbler. 50

Sherry Cocktail. 50

Sherry Wine Flip. 50

Silver Fizz. 50

Sleeper. 51

Snow Ball. 51

Snow Flake. 51

Splificator. 51

St. Charles' Punch. 51

St. Croix or Jamaica Rum Punch. 52

St. Petersburg Cocktail. 52

Stone Fence. 52

Stone Fence. 52

Strained Toddy. 52

Tea Cobbler. 52

Tea Punch. 52

The Crank's Drink. 53

Tom and Jerry. 53

Tom Gin Cocktail. 53

Trilby Cocktail. 54

Velvet Gaff. 54

Vermouth Cocktail. 54

Wachholderbeeren Hahnschwanz. 54

Wedding Punch. 54

Whiskey and Glycerine. 55

Whiskey and Mint. 55

Whiskey Cocktail. 55

Whiskey Crust. 55

Whiskey Daisy. 55

Whiskey Julep. 56

Whiskey Punch. 56

Whiskey Punch. 56

Whiskey Sangaree. 56

Whiskey Smash. 57

Whiskey Sour. 57

TEMPERANCE DRINKS. 58

Egg Lemonade. 58

Egg Lemonade. 58

Fine Lemonade for Parties. 58

Milk and Seltzer. 58

Soda Cocktail. 59

Soda Cocktail. 59

Apollinaris Lemonade. 59

Seltzer Lemonade. 59

Seltzer Lemonade. 59

Saratoga Cooler. 59

White Plush. 60

Soda Lemonade. 61

Orgeat Lemonade. 61

MISCELLANOUS 62

Wine. 62

Whiskey. 63

Brewing. 64

Health and Alcohol. 65

Recipes for Cooking. 67

- Green Sea Turtle Soup. 67
- Mock Turtle. 67
- Deviled Crabs. 67
- How to Cook a Ham Properly. 67
- Clam Chowder. 67
- Genuine English Plum Pudding. 68
- New England Bread. 68
- Tea Biscuits. 68
- Sweet Muffins. 68
- Cheese Sauce. 68
- July Dinner for Five Persons. 69
- Menu for July Dinner. 69
- Fillets of Fish. 70
- Boiled Cauliflower. 70
- Thanksgiving Dinner 70
- Champagne Punch. 71

Beverages that go with food. 72

The Model Bartender. 72

Preparation for customers. 73

Hints for young Bartenders. 73

Don'ts for young Bartenders. 74

Opening wines. 94

To Serve Champagne. 94

Cordials. 94

Syrups, Essences, Tinctures, etc. 96
- Plain Syrup. 96
- Gum Syrup. 96
- Lemon Syrup. 96
- Essence of Lemon. 96
- Tincture of Orange Peel. 97
- Tincture of Lemon Peel. 97

Tincture of Cloves. 97
Tincture of Cinnamon. 97

STOCK FOR A FIRST-CLASS BAR.

* * * *

FINE LIQUORS,

OLD WHISKEYS,

CHOICEST WINES,

FRENCH CORDIALS,

IMPORTED AND DOMESTIC ALE,

BEER AND STOUT,

IMPORTED AND DOMESTIC SODA,

A SELECT VARIETY OF SOFT DRINKS,

PURE AND POTENT SELTZER,

SCHROEDER'S, ANGOSTURA AND BOKER'S BITTERS,

THE MOST APPROVED SELECTION OF

SEASONING SPICES,

TROPICAL FRUITS,

AND THE USUAL PURE SYRUPS, ESSENCES, ETC.

THE MIXICOLOGIST,

OR,

HOW TO MIX ALL DRINKS.

"'Arf and 'Arf."

(Use metal or stone barmug.)

Mix porter or stout with ale in equal quantities, or in proportions to suit the taste.

This is the English method, and usually "draw it mild, Mary; the ale first."

A Reviver.

Put three or four lumps of ice in lemonade glass, one jigger raspberry syrup, one wineglass milk, one pony brandy; fill glass with sweet soda.

Absinthe Cocktail.

(Use Medium-size glass.)

Fill glass nearly full fine ice; cool off claret glass while preparing.

Take 2 dashes Schroeder's or Angostura bitters.

2 dashes anisette.

2/3 jigger absinthe.

Add a little water; stir well, and strain into claret glass.

Absinthe Frappe.

Fill mixing glass with fine ice, one jigger absinthe, a few drops anisette; shake well, strain in claret glass and fill with Seltzer.

Ale Sangaree.

(Use thin glass.)

Barspoonful sugar, a few drops lemon, little water to dissolve, one lump ice; pour ale in slowly. Stir carefully, filling up with the ale. Serve with a little nutmeg on top.

An Eye-opener.

In tall, thin glass put one teaspoonful Bromo Seltzer, one jigger Holland or Tom Gin (genuine), fill with club soda; drink while effervescent.

Apple Brandy Cocktail.

Fill mixing glass two thirds full of ice, small barspoonful syrup, two dashes Schroeder's bitters, three dashes Curaçao, one jigger apple brandy. Stir well; strain in cocktail glass.

Apple Toddy.

(Use medium barglass, hot.)

Take 1 large teaspoonful of fine sugar dissolved in a little boiling-hot water.

1 wineglass of brandy (applejack).

1/2 of a baked apple.

Fill the glass two thirds full of boiling water, stir up, and grate a little nutmeg on top. Serve with a spoon.

Attorney General.

(Similar to Kentucky Toddy.)

Take good-sized thick glass; two lumps cut sugar dissolve in a little water, two lumps ice, one jigger Kentucky whiskey (Laingape); stir; add one small slice lemon and little nutmeg. Serve in same glass with spoon.

B. & S.

(Use medium thin barglass.)

Take 1 pony glass of brandy.

1 small lump of ice.

Add one bottle of plain soda water. This bottle of soda will do for two split.

Beef Tea.

Put a barspoonful of the extract in a hot cup; add salt, pepper and celery salt; fill the cup with hot water, stir well, adding a few drops Worcestershire sauce and a few drops of old sherry. Serve with fine ice in glass on side.

Benedictine.

Served in the same manner as pony brandy. All Liquers served in same style except pousse-cafe.

Big 4 Mint Julep.

(Use large thin glass.)

Put some mint in glass; add a barspoonful powdered sugar; dissolve; don't crush the mint; put in some fine ice, one and a quarter jigger fine old whiskey; stir, and fill up with ice to top of glass; now place two nice sprigs of mint in glass, decorate with fruit, and lastly, a dash of St. Croix rum on top; sprinkle a little sugar on mint and serve with straws.

Bijou Cocktail.

Take 1/3 Grand Marnier.

1/3 Vermouth.

1/3 Plymouth Gin.

Mix and strain; a delicious drink. Grand Marnier can also be served in pony glass like any liquor.

Bishop.

(Use large soda glass.)

Take 1 teaspoonful of powdered white sugar dissolved in 1 wineglass of water.

2 thin slices of lemon.

2 dashes of Jamaica rum.

2 or three small lumps of ice.

Fill the glass with claret or red Burgundy; shake up well, and remove the ice before serving.

HUSS BROS. MFG. CO.

Bar Fixtures and Billiard Tables

The Largest House in the World.

John Street and Carlisle Avenue,

CINCINNATI, O.

Bowl of Claret Punch.

Four bottles of Claret. Dissolve in sufficient water 3 tablespoonfuls of powdered sugar for each bottle of Claret; slice in two lemons and two oranges, also some pineapple; pour in the claret; mix well, and just before serving put in one quart of domestic Champagne. Serve with square piece of ice in the bowl.

Brandy and Ginger Ale.

Put in thin lemonade glass

1 jigger brandy.

1 lump ice.

Fill with imported ginger ale; serve.

Brandy and Gum.

(Use small barglass.)

Take 2 dashes of gum syrup.

1 small lump of ice.

Hand the bottle to the customer and let him help himself.

Serve ice water in a separate glass.

Brandy and Mint.

Put in small barglass 1 lump cut loaf-sugar, dissolve in water.

Take 1 sprig mint, bruised slightly.

2 lumps ice.

1 jigger brandy.

Serve with small barspoon in glass; ice water on side.

Brandy and Rum Punch.

(Use large barglass.)

Take 1 tablespoonful of powdered sugar, dissolved in a little water.

1 wineglass of Santa Cruz rum.

1/2 wineglass of brandy.

Juice of half a small lemon.

1 slice of orange (cut in quarters.)

1 piece of pineapple.

Fill the tumbler with shaved ice; shake well, and dress the top with sliced lime and berries in season; serve with a straw.

Brandy and Soda.

Put two or three lumps ice in thin lemonade glass, one jigger brandy; pour in one bottle of club soda.

Brandy Cocktail.

(Use small barglass.)

Take 2 dashes syrup.

2 dashes Angostura or Schroeder's bitters.

1 jigger brandy.

Fill the glass two thirds full shaved ice; stir, and strain into cool glass with fruit in season.

Brandy Crust.

(Use small barglass.)

Take 3 or 4 dashes of gum syrup.

1 dash of Schroeder's bitters.

1 wineglass of brandy.

2 dashes of curagoa.

1 dash lemon juice.

Before inixing the above ingredients prepare a cocktail glass as follows:

Rub a sliced lemon around the rim of the glass, and dip it in pulverized white sugar, so that the sugar will adhere to the edge of the glass; pare half a lemon the same as you would an apple (all in one piece) so that the paring will fit in the wineglass; put the above ingredients into a small whiskey glass filled one third full of shaved ice; shake up well, and strain the liquid into the cocktail glass, prepared as above directed.

Brandy Daisy.

(Use small barglass.)

Take 3 or 4 dashes of gum syrup.

2 or 3 dashes of Curaçoa cordial.

The juice of half a small lemon.

1 small wineglass of brandy.

2 dashes of Jamaica rum.

Fill glass one third full of shaved ice.

Shake well, strain into a large cocktail glass, and fill up with Seltzer water from a syphon.

Brandy Fix.

Put in thin lemonade glass small barspoonful sugar, enough water to dissolve; fill half full of ice, juice one quarter lemon, four dashes pineapple syrup, one jigger brandy; stir well, fill glass full of ice, trim with seasonable fruits; serve with straws.

Brandy Fizz.

(Use medium barglass.)

Take 1 teaspoonful of powdered sugar.

3 dashes of lemon juice.

1 wineglass of brandy.

Fill with ice, shake well and strain.

Fill up the glass with Apollinaris or Seltzer water.

Brandy Flip.

Fill mixing glass two thirds full of fine ice, one barspoonful sugar, one jigger brandy, one egg; shake well; strain in star champagne glass, nutmeg on top; serve.

Brandy Julep.

Same as Big 4, using good brandy instead of whiskey.

Brandy Punch.

(Use large barglass.)

Take 1 teaspoonful of powdered sugar, dissolved in a little water.

1 wineglass of brandy.

1/2 wineglass of Jamaica rum.

Juice of half a lemon.

2 slices of orange.

1 piece of pineapple.

Fill the tumbler with shaved ice; shake up thoroughly, and dress the top with berries in season; serve with a straw.

Brandy Sangaree.

(Use medium barglass.)

Take 1/2 teaspoonful of fine white sugar dissolved in a little water.

1 wineglass of brandy.

Fill the glass one third full of shaved ice, shake up well, strain into a small glass and dash a little Port wine on top. Serve with a little grated nutmeg.

Brandy Smash.

(Use small barglass.)

Take 1 barspoonful of sugar.

2 tablespoonfuls of water.

3 or 4 sprigs of tender mint.

1 wineglass full of brandy.

Press the mint in the sugar and water to extract the flavor, add the brandy, and fill the glass two thirds full of shaved ice; stir thoroughly, and ornament with half a slice of orange and a few fresh sprigs of mint; serve with a straw.

Brandy Sour.

(Use small barglass.)

Take one large teaspoonful of powdered white sugar, dissolved in a little Apollinaris or seltzer water.

The juice of half a lemon.

1 dash of Curaçoa.

1 wineglass of brandy.

Fill the glass with shaved ice, shake, and strain into a claret glass. Ornament with orange and berries.

Brandy Sour.

Fill mixing glass two thirds full of fine ice, juice one quarter lemon, one dash Jamaica rum, one large spoonful sugar; shake well; strain in punch glass; add fruit.

Brandy Toddy.

Fill mixing glass two thirds full of fine ice, large barspoonful syrup, one jigger brandy; stir well and strain into previously cool cocktail glass; add a little nutmeg.

Buffalo.

(Use small goblet.)

And serve same as the foregoing recipe.

Burnt Brandy.

Put 1 lump sugar in saucer.

1 jigger brandy.

Light it with a match, let it burn for a minute or so, extinguish the flame, put in whiskey glass and serve.

Catawba Cobbler.

(Use large barglass.)

Take 2 teaspoonfuls of fine white sugar, dissolved in a little water.

1 slice of orange cut into quarters.

Fill the glass half full of shaved ice, then fill it up with catawba wine. Ornament the top with berries in season, and serve with straws.

Champagne Cobbler.

(Use bottle of wine to four large barglasses.)

Put in tall, thin glass two lumps sugar, one slice orange, one piece twisted lemon peel, fill two thirds full shaved ice, fill balance with wine; stir moderately, ornament in a tasty manner, and serve with straws.

Champagne Cocktail — (Plain.)

Put one lump cut-loaf sugar in small, thin lemonade glass, one or two dashes Schroeder's bitters, one piece twisted lemon peel; put two or three small lumps of ice; fill with champagne; stir gently; serve.

Champagne Cup.

Mix in punchbowl

1 quart champagne.

1 bottle club soda.

1 pony glass Curaçoa.

2 slices cucumber rind.

A few strawberries, if in season.

3 or 4 slices pineapple.

Serve in star champagne glasses.

Champagne Julep.

Use thin lemonade glass, one lump cut-loaf sugar, two or three small lumps of ice, two sprigs mint bruised slightly; pour in the champagne slowly; stir gently until full; add seasonable fruits; serve.

Champagne Punch.

(One quart of punch.)

Take 1 quart bottle of champagne wine.

3 tablespoonfuls of sugar.

1 orange, sliced.

the juice of a lemon.

2 slices of pineapple, cut in small pieces.

1 wineglass of raspberry or strawberry syrup.

Ornament with fruits in season, and serve in champagne goblets.

This can be made in any quantity by observing the proportions of the ingredients as given above. Four bottles of wine make a gallon, and a gallon is generally sufficient for fifteen persons in a mixed party.

Chocolate Cocktail.

(Use large lemonade glass.)

Fill with ice.

Take 1 barspoonful of sugar.

1 egg.

1/2 jigger mariaschino.

1/2 jigger chartreuse.

Shake well, and strain in cocktail glass.

Claret Cobbler.

(Use large barglass.)

This drink is made the same way as the catawba cobbler, using claret wine instead of catawba, and is a very refreshing drink.

Claret Cup.

Take 1 bottle of claret.

little water.

1 tablespoonful of powdered sugar.

1 teaspoonful of powdered cinnamon, cloves, and allspice, mixed.

1/2 lemon.

1 bottle soda.

Mix the ingredients well together, adding the thin rind of cucumber and some mint, not pressed. This is a nice summer beverage for evening parties.

Claret Flip.

Fill mixing glass two thirds full of fine ice, large barspoonful sugar, two jiggers claret, one egg; shake well, strain in star champagne glass, nutmeg on top.

Claret Punch.

(Use good-sized glass.)

Nearly fill with claret.

1 piece of lemon peel.

Put in thin lemonade glass one large spoonful sugar, sufficient water to dissolve; fill half full of fine ice; stir well, trim with fruits, serve with straws.

Coffee Cobbler.

(Use large lemonade glass.)

Fill glass two two thirds with ice, one desert teaspoonful powdered sugar; stir, then pour in one jigger brandy; stir thoroughly. Serve with straws. An excellent stimulant.

Coffee Cocktail.

(Use large barglass.)

Fill two thirds full ice.

1 spoonful sugar.

1 egg.

1/2 jigger sherry.

1/2 jigger port.

Shake thoroughly, and strain, with nutmeg on top.

Creme de Menthe.

Fill sherry glass with fine ice, pour in Creme de Menthe over the ice until glass is full; serve with one straw in glass.

Curaçoa Punch.

(Use large barglass.)

Take one tablespoonful of powdered white sugar, dissolved in a little water.

1 wineglass of brandy.

1/4 wineglass of Jamaica rum.

1/2 pony glass of Curaçoa.

the juice of half a lemon.

Fill the tumbler with shaved ice, shake well, and ornament with fruits of the season. Serve with a straw.

Dripped Absinthe.

Put pony glass in mixing glass, fill around with fine ice, fill pony with absinthe, drip about two jiggers water throug hdrip in absinthe, running over the sides of pony; then take out pony and stir; strain in port wine glass.

Duke of Norfolk Punch.

(For bottling.)

Take 2 quarts of brandy.

1 quart of white wine.

1 quart of milk.

1¼ pounds of sugar.

6 lemons.

3 oranges.

Pare off the peel of the oranges and lemons very thin; put the peel and all the juice into a vessel with a close-fitting lid. Pour on the brandy, wine and milk, and add the sugar after having dissolved in sufficient water. Mix well, and cover close for twenty-four hours. Strain until clear, and bottle.

Parties at a distance requiring any number of copies of this book will address

C. F. LAWLOR,

Burnet House, Cincinnati, Ohio.

Durkee.

(Use large glass.)

Put in mixing glass one lemon with peel on; one spoonful sugar; muddle well; fill two thirds full fine ice, one jigger Jamaica rum, one pony Curaçoa; fill with club soda; carefully stir and strain. This will serve for two split.

Dutch Cocktail.

(Use large goblet.)

One third full of beer.

One bottle ordinary mineral water.

This is a very good drink for stopping thirst. It is universally known.

Egg Sour.

(Use small barglass.)

Take 1 teaspoonful of powdered sugar.

3 dashes of lemon juice.

1 pony of Curaçoa.

1 pony of brandy.

1 egg.

2 or 3 small lumps of ice.

Shake up well, and remove the ice before serving.

Eggnog in Quantity.

Two and a half gallons. Separate the whites from the yolks of one dozen eggs, whip them separately — the whites until very stiff, the yolks until very thin; put the yolks in large bowl, add three pounds powdered sugar, stirring constantly to prevent sugar from lumping, three pints brandy, one pint Jamaica rum, two gallons rich milk. While stirring put in an ounce of nutmeg. If not strong enough to suit, add more brandy, then put the whites on top. When serving, cut off a small quantity of white and put on top of glass with a dash of nutmeg.

Eggnog.

(Use large barglass.)

Take 1 large teaspoonful of powdered sugar.

1 fresh egg.

1/2 wineglass of brandy.

1/2 wineglass of Santa Cruz rum.

A little shaved ice.

Fill the glass with rich milk, and shake up the ingredients until they are thoroughly mixed. Pour the mixture into a goblet, excluding the ice, and grate a little nutmeg on top. This may be made by using a wineglass of either of the above liquors, instead of both combined.

English Bishop.

(To make one quart.)

Take 1 quart of Port wine.

1 orange (stuck pretty well with cloves, the quantity being a matter of taste).

Roast the orange before a fire, and when suffi- ciently brown, cut it in quarters, and pour over it a quart of Port wine (previously made hot), add sugar to taste, and let the mixture simmer over the fire for half an hour.

Gin Crust.

(Use small barglass.)

Gin crust is made like the brandy crust, using gin instead of brandy.

Gin Daisy.

In same manner as whiskey, only using gin.

Gin Fizz.

(Use medium barglass.)

Take 1 teaspoonful of powdered sugar.

3 dashes of lemon juice.

1 wineglass of Old Tom gin.

Fill with ice, shake well and strain.

Fill up the glass with Apollinaris or Seltzer water, stir thoroughly and serve.

Gin Julep.

(Use large barglass.)

The gin julep is made with the same ingredients as the mint julep, omitting the fancy fixings.

Gin Sangaree.

Same as brandy or whiskey sangaree, substituting Holland or Old Tom gin instead of brandy or whiskey.

Gin Smash.

(Use small barglass.)

Take 1 barspoonful of sugar.

2 teaspoonfuls of water.

1 wineglass of gin.

3 or 4 sprigs of tender mint.

Put the mint in the glass, then the sugar and water; inash the mint to extract the flavor; add the gin, and fill up the glass with shaved ice; stir up well, and ornament with two or three fresh sprigs of mint.

Golden Fizz.

Same as Silver Fizz, using the yolkin place of the white of an egg.

Bear in mind all fizzes and similar drinks must be taken while effervescing or they lose their natural taste.

Golden Slipper.

Put in bell-shape claret glass half jigger yellow Chartreuse, yolk of one egg, fill with Kirsch Wasser.

Half and Half.

(Use metal or slone barmug.)

Mix half old and half new ale together. This is the American method.

Half and Half. (Dublin Style.)

Fill ale glass one half with ale and the other with stout.

Hendrick Cocktail.

(Use old-fashioned toddy glass.)

Fill two thirds full ice.

Take 2 dashes syrup.

2 dashes Schroeder's bitters.

1 dash absinthe.

1 jigger old Kentucky bourbon.

1 small slice lemon.

Stir, and serve in the same glass without straining.

High Ball.

Put in thin ale glass one lump of ice; fill with syphon seltzer to within an inch of the top, then float one half jigger brandy or whiskey.

Hints on Using Ice.

Great care should be used in handling ice. Do not use the hands. Sometimes a customer asks for more ice. Use spoon or silver scoop. See that your ice is perfectly clean and properly shaved, also having some lumps arranged according to demand for different drinks.

Hock Cobbler.

(Use large barglass.)

This drink is made the same way as the catawba cobbler, using Hock wine instead of catawba.

Hot Brandy.

In hot whiskey glass put one lump cut-loaf sugar, enough hot water to dissolve, one jigger brandy; fill glass to within half an inch of the top with hot water, nutmeg on top; serve with spoon in glass.

Hot Eggnog.

(Use large barglass.)

This drink is very popular in California, and is made in precisely the same manner as the cold eggnog above, except that you must use boiling water instead of ice.

Hot English Ale Flip.

(One quart.)

This is prepared in the same manner as the Rum Flip, omitting the rum and the whites of two of the eggs.

Hot English Rum Flip.

(One quart.)

Take 1 quart of ale.

1 gill of old rum.

4 raw fresh eggs.

4 ounces of moist sugar.

Heat the ale in a sausepan; beat up the eggs and sugar, add the nutmeg and rum, and put it all in a pitcher. When the ale is near to a boil, put it in another pitcher; pour it very gradually in the pitcher containing the eggs, etc., stirring all the while very briskly to prevent the eggs from curdling; then pour the contents of the two pitchers from one to the other until the mixture is as smooth as cream.

Hot Irish Whiskey Punch.

(Use medium barglass.)

Take 1 wineglass Kinahan's or Jamieson's Irish whiskey.

2 wineglasses of boiling water.

2 lumps of loaf-sugar.

Dissolve the sugar well with one wineglass of the water, then pour in the whiskey, add the balance of the water, and put in a small piece of lemon peel. Before using the glass rinse it in hot water.

Hot Milk Punch.

(Use large barglass.)

This punch is made the same as the above, with the exception that hot milk is used, and no ice.

Hot Scotch Whiskey Punch.

(Use medium barglass.)

Take 1 wineglass of Glenlivet or Islay whiskey.

2 wineglasses of boiling water.

Sugar to taste.

Dissolve the sugar with one wineglass of the water, then pour in the whiskey, add the balance of the water, and put in a small piece of lemon peel. Before using the glass rinse it in hot water.

Hot Spiced Rum.

(Use medium barglass, hot.)

Take 1 small teaspoonful of powdered white sugar.

1 wineglass of Jamaica rum.

1 teaspoonful of spices (allspice and cloves, not ground).

1 piece of sweet butter as large as half a chestnut.

Dissolve the sugar in a little boiling water, add the rum, spices, and butter, and fill the glass two thirds full of boiling water.

Hot Rum.

(Use medium barglass, hot.)

Take 1 lump of cut sugar.

1 wineglass of Jamaica rum.

1 piece of sweet butter as large as half a chestnut.

Dissolve the sugar in a little boiling water, add the rum and butter, fill the glass two thirds full of boiling water, stir, grate a little nutmeg on top, and serve.

Hot Whiskey Sling.

(Use medium barglass, hot.)

Take 1 small teaspoonful of powdered sugar.

1 wineglass of bourbon or rye whiskey.

Dissolve the sugar in a little hot water, add the whiskey, and fill the glass two thirds full of boiling water; grate a little nutmeg on top and serve.

How to Serve Tom and Jerry.

(Use T. and J. Mug.)

Take 1 desertspoonful of the above mixture.

1 wineglass of brandy or whiskey.

Fill the glass with boiling water, grate a little nutmeg on top, and serve with a spoon.

Improved Brandy Cocktail.

(Use ordinary barglass.)

Take 2 dashes Schroeder's or Angostura.

2 dashes gum syrup.

2 dashes maraschino

1 dash absinthe.

7/8 jigger brandy.

Stir well, and strain with fruit and twisted lemon peel in a cool champagne glass.

Improved Tom Gin Cocktail.

(Use medium-size glass.)

Fill with fine ice.

Take 1 dash Curaçoa.

2 dashes bitters (some preferring orange only).

1 jigger Old Tom.

Stir well, and strain in cool cocktail glass.

Improved Whiskey Cocktail.

Prepared in the same manner as the Improved Brandy Cocktail, by substituting rye or bourbon whiskey for the brandy.

Irish Cocktail.

(Use large glass.)

Take 1 lump ice.

2 drops Schroeder's or Boker's bitters.

1/2 naggin Irish whiskey.

1 bottle C. & C. ginger ale.

This is a very palatable drink, and is the favorite of the Irish members of Parliament.

John Collins.

Put in mixing glass one half lemon with peel on; one spoonful sugar; muddle well; fill glass two thirds full of shaved ice, one jigger Old Tom gin; shake well; strain in thin lemonade glass; fill with club soda; stir.

K and K Punch.

Put in mixing glass one barspoonful sugar, one quarter lemon with peel on; muddle well; fill two thirds full of fine ice, one jigger whiskey; fill with Apollinaris; stir with spoon thoroughly; strain in ale glass previously cooled; add fruit.

Kentucky Toddy.

Same as old-fashioned toddy, adding little lemon peel.

La Casino Fizz.

Fill lemonade glass with fine ice to cool it. Put in mixing glass two thirds fine ice, juice one quarter lemon, one barspoonful sugar, three dashes Curaçao, white of one egg; shake well, strain, fill with syphon Seltzer.

Lawlor's Pousse Cafe.

(Use a small wineglass.)

Take 1/4 Curaçoa.

1/4 maraschino.

1/4 yellow chartreuse.

1/4 old Cognac brandy.

Keep all the ingredients separate. See concluding remarks in the preceding recipe.

Lemonade.

This drink, although simple in name, is very important in first class bars. One good-sized lemon, peeled, cut in half, one and one half large spoonfuls sugar, the lemon well pressed; fill glass two thirds full of ice, fill with water, and shake thoroughly, and strain carefully into thin glass, or serve with straws, adding fruit according to customer's wish. Can be made sour, and with Apollinaris or Seltzer according to order.

Manhattan Cocktail.

(Medium-size glass.)

Take 1 dash Schroeders bitters.

1 half barspoonful syrup.

1 half jigger vermouth.

1 half jigger whiskey.

2 dashes of maraschino.

Stir well in glass previously filled with fine ice; strain in cool cocktail glass.

Manhattan Milk Punch.

Same as the *Cold* Milk Punch, with the addition of five drops of aromatic tincture.

Martinez Cocktail.

(Use medium-size glass.)

Take 2 dashes orange bitters.

1 dash syrup.

1/2 jigger Old Tom gin.

1/2 jigger vermouth.

Stir well, and strain into cocktail glass; add one imported cherry.

Milk Punch.

Fill large mixing glass half full of ice.

Take 1 large spoonful of sugar.

1 jigger brandy.

4 or 5 dashes rum.

Fill the glass with milk, shake well, strain in tall, thin lemonade glass, nutmeg on top.

Milk Punch.

(Use large barglass.)

Take 1 desertspoonful of fine sugar.

1 wineglass of brandy.

1/2 wineglass Santa Cruz rum.

1/2 glass fine ice.

Fill with milk, shake the ingredients well together, strain into a large glass, and grate a little nutmeg on top.

Morning Cocktail.

(Use medium-size glass.)

Take 3 dashes syrup.

2 dashes Curaçoa.

2 dashes Schroeder's or Boker's bitters.

1 dash absinthe.

1 pony brandy.

1 pony whiskey.

Stir well, and strain into long, thin glass, filling it up with fresh apollinaris, and stir with a spoon having a little sugar in it.

Old-fashioned Cocktail.

Crush in small barglass one lump loaf sugar, put in two dashes Schroeder's bitters, one piece twisted lemon peel, two or three small lumps of ice, one jigger whiskey. Serve with small barspoon in glass.

Old-fashioned Punch.

(Use medium-sized glass.)

Made with same ingredients as the foregoing, excepting to stir with spoon and serve with the ice in same glass with a strainer or straws.

Old-fashioned Toddy.

(Use thick glass.)

One good-sized lump sugar, dissolve with a little water, one lump ice, one jigger whiskey; stir; add nutmeg and serve in same glass.

Parisian Pousse Cafe.

(Use small wineglass.)

Take 2/5 Curaçoa.

2/5 Kirschwasser.

1/5 chartreuse.

Care should be taken to keep the ingredients from mixing together. See preceding recipes.

Pineapple Julep.

(For a party of five.)

Take the juice of two oranges.

1 gill of raspberry syrup.

1 gill of Maraschino.

1 gill of Old Tom gin.

1 quart bottle of sparkling Moselle.

1 ripe pineapple, peeled, sliced, and cut up.

Put all the materials in a glass bowl; ice, and serve in flat glasses, ornamented with berries in season.

Plain Lemonade.

(Use large barglass.)

Take the juice of half a large lemon.

1½ tablespoonfuls of sugar.

2 or 3 pieces of orange.

Shake, and serve with straws.

Pony Brandy.

To serve pony brandy properly, take whiskey glass, set it on counter top downwards, place pony on top, place 1 small lump ice in a whiskey glass,

fill pony with only finest Cognac. Customer can Take 1t plain or he will pour it on the ice at his optiou.

Port Wine Flip.

(Use large barglass.)

Take 1 barspoonful of powdered sugar.

1 large wineglass of Port wine.

1 fresh egg.

Glass two thirds full of ice.

Break the egg into the glass, add the sugar, and lastly the wine and ice. Shake up thoroughly, and strain into a medium-sized goblet; nutmeg on top.

Port Wine Sangaree.

Fill mixing glass half full of fine ice.

1 barspoonful sugar.

1 piece lemon peel.

1 jigger port wine.

Shake well, strain in star champagne glass, nutmeg on top.

Whiskey, brandy, and gin in the same manner.

Porter Cup.

Take 1 bottle of porter.

1 bottle of ale.

1 glass of brandy.

1 dessertspoonful of syrup of ginger.

3 or 4 lumps of sugar.

1/2 nutmeg, grated.

1 teaspoonful carbonate of soda.

1 cucumber.

Mix the porter and ale in a covered jug; add the brandy, syrup of ginger, and nutmeg; cover it, and expose it to the cold for half an hour. When serving, put in the carbonate of soda.

Porter Sangaree.

(Use thin glass.)

Same as Ale Sangaree, using porter.

Pousse l'Amour.

(Use a sherry glass.)

Take 1/2 glass of maraschino.

Yolk of 1 egg.

Sufficient vanilla cordial to surround the egg.

1 tablespoonful of fine old brandy.

First; pour in the maraschino, then introduce the yolk with a spoon, without disturbing the maraschino; next carefully surround the egg with vanilla cordial, and lastly put the brandy on top.

In making a Pousse of any kind the greatest care should be observed to keep all the ingredients composing it separate. This may best be accomplished by pouring the different materials from a sherry wine glass. It requires a steady hand and careful manipulation to succeed in making a perfect Pousse.

Punch a la Dwyer.

In punchbowl put —

1 dozen lumps cut loaf sugar.

1 lemon sliced.

1 orange sliced thin.

1 quart Burgundy.

2 jiggers 1835 Cognac.

1 quart Apollinaris.

1 quart champagne.

1 large lump ice.

Stir together; serve.

Punch a la Romaine.

(For a party of fifteen.)

Take 1 bottle of rum.

1 bottle of wine.

10 lemons.

2 sweet oranges.

2 pounds of powdered sugar.

10 eggs.

Dissolve the sugar in the juice of the lemons and oranges, adding the thin rind of one orange; strain through a sieve into a bowl, and add by degrees the whites of the eggs beaten to a froth. Place the bowl on ice for a while, then stir in briskly the rum and the wine.

Remsen Cooler.

Pare the rind from a lemon, leaving the rind whole; put it in a large punch glass with two or three small lumps ice and a jigger Old Tom gin; fill up with plain soda.

Rhine Wine and Seltzer.

(Use medium thin glass.)

Fill half full or little better of wine, balance Seltzer or Apolinaris. Any still wine in same manner. Ice if wanted, only in lump. Regulate according to customer's desire.

Rhine Wine Cobbler.

(Use large barglass.)

The same as catawba using Rhine wine.

Rickey.

Take nice thin goblet, one lump ice, squeeze juice of one good-sized lime or two small ones, one jigger Old Tom Gin. Fill up with Club soda, stir, and serve with spoon in goblet.

Rock and Rye.

(Use whiskey glass.)

Barspoonful rock candy syrup, small spoon in glass. Let customer help himself to whiskey. This is the best R. and R. Also honey can be used, only dissolving honey well before the liquor is poured in.

Roman Punch.

(Use large barglass.)

Take one tablespoonful of powdered white sugar, dissolved in a little water.

1 tablespoonful of raspberry syrup.

1 teaspoonful of Curaçoa.

1 wineglass of Jamaica rum.

1/2 wineglass of brandy, the juice of half a lemon.

Fill with shaved ice, shake well, dash with port wine, and ornament with fruits in season. Serve with a straw.

Rum Sour.

Fill mixing glass two thirds full of fine ice, juice one quarter lemon, large spoonful syrup, one jigger N. E., Jamaica or St. Croix rum; shake well. Strain in star Champagne glass with fruit.

Sauterne Cobbler.

(Use large barglass.)

The same as catawba cobbler, using sauterne instead of catawba.

Shandy Gaff.

(Use large barglass, or mug.)

Fill the glass half full of ale, and the remaining half with Irish ginger ale.

In England, where this drink had its origin, it is made with Bass' ale and ginger ale, half and half.

Sheridan Punch or Float.

Strain lemonade in thin lemonade glass to within an inch of top, float over a spoon one half jigger of whiskey on lemonade.

Sherry and Bitters.

(Use sherry wineglass.)

Take one dash of Schroeder's bitters, twist the glass around so that the bitters will cover the whole surface of the glass. Fill with sherry wine and serve.

Sherry and Egg.

(Use small barglass.)

Pour in glass a little sherry. Break in the glass one fresh egg. Then fill with sherry.

Sherry and Ice.

(Use small barglass.)

Put in the glass two or three small lumps of ice.

Place the decanter of wine before customer.

Sherry Cobbler.

(Use large barglass.)

Take 1 tablespoonful powdered sugar.
1 slice orange cut in 2 parts.
Dissolve sugar.

Fill the glass with shaved ice, then fill it up with sherry wine; stir it carefully, ornament the top with pineapple and berries and serve with straws.

Sherry Cocktail.

(Use small mixing glass.)

Made in same manner as whiskey, only using Amontillada sherry.

Sherry Wine Flip.

(Use large barglass.)

This is made precisely as the Port wine flip, substituting sherry wine instead of Port.

Silver Fizz.

(Use large barglass.)

Take 1 tablespoonful of pulverized sugar.

3 dashes of lemon or lime juice.

The white of one egg.

1 wineglass of Old Tom gin.

2 or 3 small lumps of ice.

Shake up thoroughly, strain into a medium barglass, and fill it up with Seltzer water.

Sleeper.

Take 1 gill of old rum.

1 ounce of sugar.

2 raw fresh eggs.

1/2 pint of water.

Mix well.

Snow Ball.

Place on the bar a large lemonade glass full of fine ice, putting in a mixing glass one half tablespoonful fine sugar, half jigger whiskey and white of one egg. Fill three fourths with fine ice; shake well and strain into the lemonade glass, after throwing out the ice; then fill with imported ginger ale.

Snow Flake.

(Use thin glass.)

Take large thin glass half filled with sweet milk; fill up with Imperial or seltzer water; both ingredients must be cold.

Splificator.

(Use medium thin glass.)

One piece ice; let customer help himself to whiskey, and fill up with Apollinaris water.

St. Charles' Punch.

(Use large barglass.)

Take 1 teaspoonful of powdered sugar, dissolved in a little water.

1 wine glass of Port wine.

1 pony glass of brandy.

The juice of quarter of a lemon.

Fill the tumbler with shaved ice, shake well, ornament with fruits in season, and serve with a straw.

St. Croix or Jamaica Rum Punch.

In same manner as whiskey punch.

St. Petersburg Cocktail.

Fill glass with fine ice, using medium-size thin glass or goblet; then empty out ice; now fill with sugar, empty again; now put in two lumps ice, two thirds jigger brandy, piece twisted lemon peel; fill up with champagne.

Stone Fence.

Serve the same as plain whiskey, substituting cider for water on the side.

Stone Fence.

Whiskey with cider on side instead water.

Strained Toddy.

Put in mixing glass one barspoonful sugar, one quarter lemon with peel on; muddle; fill glass two thirds full of shaved ice, one jigger whiskey, one jigger water, stir well, strain in star champagne glass, nutmeg on top.

Tea Cobbler.

(Use large lemonade glass.)

Made in same manner as Coffee Cobbler, using Irish whiskey instead of brandy, with a thin slice lemon added.

Tea Punch.

(Use heated metal bowl.)

Take 1/2 pint of good brandy.

1/2 pint of rum.

1/4 pound of loaf-sugar, dissolved in water.

1 ounce of best green tea.

1 quart of boiling water.

1 large lemon.

Infuse the tea in the water. Warm a silver or other metal bowl until quite hot; place in it the brandy, rum, sugar, and the juice of the lemon. The oil of the lemon peel should be first obtained by rubbing with a few lumps of the sugar. Set the contents of the bowl on fire; and while flaming, pour in the tea gradually, stirring with a ladle. It will continue to burn for some time, and should be ladled into glasses while in that condition. A heated metal bowl will cause the punch to burn longer than if a china bowl is used.

The Crank's Drink.

ON THE WAGNER SLEEPER.

2/8 brandy.

5/8 whiskey.

1/8 port wine.

Tom and Jerry.

(Use punch-bowl for the mixture.)

Take 12 fresh eggs.

1/2 small barglass of Jamaica rum.

1½ teaspoonfuls of ground cinnamon.

1/2 teaspoonful of ground cloves.

1/2 teaspoonful of ground allspice.

Sufficient fine white sugar.

Beat the whites of the eggs to a stiff froth, and the yolks until they are as thin as water; then mix together, and add the spice and rum; stir up thoroughly, and thicken with sugar until the mixture attains the consistence of a light batter.

Tom Gin Cocktail.

Fill mixing glass two thirds full of shaved ice.

1 or 2 dashes Boker's or Schroeder's bitters.

1 barspoonful syrup.

1 jigger Tom gin.

Stir and strain in cooled cocktail glass, twist a piece of lemon peel over the top to flavor, serve fruit if desired.

Trilby Cocktail.

(Use medium-size glass.)

Fill with shaved ice.

2 dashes raspberry syrup.

1/3 jigger vermouth.

2/3 fine brandy.

1 dash orange bitters.

Stir well, and strain into tall, fancy glass, with fruit in season.

Velvet Gaff.

One pint of Champagne, one pint of Dublin Stout, mixed in a bowl or pitcher. Serve in star Champagne glasses.

Vermouth Cocktail.

(Use large barglass.)

Fill glass two thirds full fine ice.

Take 2 dashes maraschino.

2 dashes Angostura or Schroeder's bitters.

1 jigger vermouth.

Stir, and strain into cocktail glass; fruit if desired.

Wachholderbeeren Hahnschwanz.

Prepared in same manner, using two dashes syrup instead of Curaçoa and Holland gin.

Wedding Punch.

Take 1/2 pint of pineapple juice.

1 pint of lemon juice.

1 pint of lemon syrup.

1 pint of claret or port wine.

1/2 pound of sugar.

1/2 pint of boiling water.

6 grains of vanilla.

1 grain of ambergris.

1 pint of strong brandy.

Rub the vanilla and ambergris with the sugar in the brandy thoroughly; let it stand in a corked bottle for a few hours, shaking occasionally. Then add the lemon juice, pineapple juice and wine; filter through flannel, and lastly add the syrup.

Whiskey and Glycerine.

Half tablespoonful pure glycerine, one jigger of whiskey. This is a most excellent remedy for a cold or any disease of the throat or lungs. When possible, it should be taken a spoonful at a time at intervals of a half hour, letting it trickle down the throat. If the taste is not agreeable, a teaspoonful of wintergreen essence will make it palatable.

Whiskey and Mint.

Put in barglass one lump cut-loaf sugar, enough water to dissolve, one or two sprigs mint; mash sugar and mint together; serve same as plain whiskey, leaving barspoon in glass.

Whiskey Cocktail.

(Use medium-size glass.)

Fill glass two thirds full of fine ice; small barspoonful of syrup; two dashes Schroeder's bitters, 1 jigger whiskey. Stir well; strain in cooled cocktail glass; squeeze the oil from a piece lemon peel on top fruit if desired.

Whiskey Crust.

(Use small barglass.)

The whiskey crust is made in the same manner as the brandy crust, using whiskey instead of brandy.

Whiskey Daisy.

(Use small barglass.)

Take 3 dashes of gum syrup.

2 dashes syrup.

The juice of half a small lemon.

1 wineglass of bourbon or rye whiskey.

Fill glass one third full of shaved ice.

Shake well, strain into a large cocktail glass, and fill up with Seltzer, Apollinaris or Imperial water.

Whiskey Julep.

(Use large barglass.)

The whiskey julep is made the same as the mint julep, omitting all fruits and berries.

Whiskey Punch.

(Use lemonade glass.)

Take quarter of a lemon, one barspoonful sugar, little water; press the lemon; one jigger bourbon or rye whiskey, fill glass with ice, two dashes rum; shake well and strain into cool stem punch glass, add fruit. Two or three punches can be made in large glass at the same time, first filling up your stem glasses with ice for as many as required. This is one of the best ways to make a good whiskey punch.

Whiskey Punch.

(Chicago style.)

Take two same sized mixing glasses, fill with ice, put four dashes syrup, four dashes lemon, one jigger whiskey in one of the mixing glasses; place the other on top, reversing until cold, then strain from both into cool glass, holding them firmly; add fruit.

Whiskey Sangaree.

(Use medium barglass.)

Same as brandy sangaree, only using rye or bourbon whiskey instead of the brandy.

Whiskey Smash.

(Use small barglass.)

Take 1 barspoonful of sugar.

2 teaspoonfuls of water.

3 or 4 sprigs of young mint.

1 wineglass of whiskey.

Proceed exactly as directed in the last recipe.

Whiskey Sour.

(Use small barglass.)

Take one large teaspoonful of powdered white sugar, dissolved in a little Seltzer or Apollinaris water.

The juice of half a small lemon.

1 wineglass of bourbon or rye whiskey.

Fill the glass full of shaved ice, shake up and strain into a claret glass. Ornament with berries.

TEMPERANCE DRINKS.

Egg Lemonade.

Same as plain, putting in egg only; shake longer.

Egg Lemonade.

(Use large barglass.)

Take 1 large tablespoonful of pulverized white sugar.

Juice of half a lemon.

1 fresh egg.

2 or 3 small lumps of ice.

Shake up thoroughly, strain into a sodawater glass and fill up the glass with soda or seltzer water. Ornament with berries.

Fine Lemonade for Parties.

(One gallon.)

Take the rind of 8 lemons.

Juice of 12 lemons.

2 pounds of loaf sugar.

1 gallon boiling water.

Rub the rinds of the eight lemons on the sugar until it has absorbed all the oil from them, and put it with the remainder of the sugar into a jug; add the lemon juice (but no pips), and pour over the whole the boiling water. When the sugar is dissolved strain the lemonade through a piece of muslin, and when cool it will be ready for use. The lemonade will be much improved by having the whites of four eggs beaten up with it. A larger or smaller quantity of this can be made by increasing or diminishing the ingredients used.

Milk and Seltzer.

(Use large soda glass.)

Fill the glass half full of milk, and the remaining half with seltzer water.

Soda Cocktail.

(Use large soda glass.)

Take 1 barspoonful sugar.

2 dashes Boker's or Schroeder's bitters.

3 lumps ice (not fine).

1 bottle soda plain (or lemon).

Serve in same glass, with spoon.

Soda Cocktail.

Take lemonade glass two thirds full of ice, one desertspoonful of sugar, two dashes Schroeder's bitters, lemon peel, bottle Trilby soda water; stir, and. serve in same glass.

Apollinaris Lemonade.

(Use lemonade glass.)

Mash one whole lemon, one large spoonful sugar, half fill with ice, fill up with the Apollinaris water; stir, and strain into thin glass, adding fruit.

Seltzer Lemonade.

Put 1 peeled lemon, cut in two, in large mixing glass, 1 large barspoonful sugar, muddle thoroughly, fill half full of ice, fill with Seltzer, stir with spoon, strain in thin glass, add fruit.

Seltzer Lemonade.

In same manner as Apollinaris, using Seltzer or Imperial water, the last being a very fine water known as Wagner's Imperial.

Saratoga Cooler.

(Use large barglass.)

Take 1 teaspoonful of powdered white sugar.

Juice of half a lemon.

1 bottle of ginger ale.

2 small lumps of ice.

Stir well, and remove the ice before serving.

White Plush.

(Use small barglass.)

Hand a bottle of bourbon or rye whiskey to the customer and let him help himself. Fill up the glass with fresh milk.

A curious story about the origin of this drink is thus told by the New York *Herald*:

" There are some mixed drinks that are standbys, and are always popular, such as cocktails, punches, and juleps; but every little while there will be a new racket sprung ou the public that will have a great run for a time, and then get knocked out by another. About a month ago white plush got its start in this way: There was a country buyer down from New England somewhere, and a party of dry goods men were trying to make it pleasant for him. So they took him into a swell barroom down town, and were going to open sour wine. Same old story, you know; get him full as a balloon and then work him for a big order. It turned out that this countryman was not such a flat as they thought him. Though he had been swigging barrels of hard cider and smuggled Canada whiskey for the last twenty years, he pleaded the temperance business on them; said he never drank, and he guessed he'd just take a glass of water if they'd git him one, as he was kinder thirsty walkin' round so much. Well, that was a set-back for the boys. They knew he had lots of money to spend, and he was one of those unapproachable ducks that have got to be warmed up before you can do anything with them.

" ' Oh, take something,' they said; ' take some milk.'

" ' Well, I guess a glass of milk would go sorter good,' said he.

" Some one suggested kumyss, and told him what it was. As they did not have any kumyss in the place they gave him some milk and seltzer. That's about the same thing. One of the boys gave the bartender a wink, and he put a dash of whiskey in it. The old man did not get on to it at all. He thought it was the seltzer that flavored it. The next round the seltzer was left out altogether and more whiskey put in. They kept on giving it to him until he got pretty well set up. It's a very insidious and seductive drink. Pretty soon the countryman got funny and tipped his glass over on the table. As it spread around he said:

" ' Gosh, it looks like white plush, don't it?'

" ' So it does,' said the boys. ' Give the gentleman another yard of white plush, here;' and the name has stuck to it ever since."

Soda Lemonade.

(Use large soda glass.)

Take 1 tablespoonful of powdered white sugar.

Juice of half a lemon.

1 bottle of plain sodawater.

2 or 3 small lumps of ice.

Stir up well, and serve with straws or strain.

SELTZER LEMONADE may be made by substituting Seltzer water for the soda.

Orgeat Lemonade.

(Use large barglass.)

Take 1 tablespoonful of powdered white sugar.

½ wineglass of orgeat syrup.

The juice of half a lemon.

Fill the tumbler one third full of fine ice, balance water. Shake well, and ornament with berries in season. Serve.

THE H. & S. POGUE CO.,

FOR

Reliable Dry Goods at Lowest Prices

20-28 W. Fourth St.,

CINCINNATI, O.

MISCELLANOUS.

Wine.

The word "wine," in its wildest sense, includes all alcoholic beverages derived from sacchariferous vegetable juices by spontaneous fermentation. In the narrower sense of its ordinary acceptance, it designates the fermented product of grape juice, with which alone the present article proposes to deal. Wine making is an easy art where there is a sufficient supply of perfectly ripe grapes. In Italy, Spain, Greece, and other countries of Southern Europe, nature takes care of this. In the more northern districts of France, and especially on the Rhine in Germany, the culture of the vine means hard work from one end of the year to the other, which only exceptionally finds its full reward. And yet it is in those naturally less favored districts that the most generous wines are produced. Southern wines excel in body and strength, but even the best of them lack the beautiful aroma or bouquet characteristic of high-class Rhine wine. The large proportion of sugar in Southern grape juice would appear to be inimical to the development of that superior flavor. To secure the highest attainable degree of maturity in the grape, the vintage on the Rhine is postponed until the grapes almost begin to wither, and the white grapes on the sunny side of the bunches exhibit a yellowish brown (instead of a green) color, and show signs of flacidity. In Spain, France, and Portugal it is a very common practice to dust over the grapes with plaster of paris, or to add the plaster to the must. The intention is to prevent putrefaction of the berries in the latter, to add to the chemical stability of the wine.

Effervescing or Sparkling Wines.

These wines are largely impregnated with carbonic acid, engendered by an after-fermentation in the closed bottle by means of added sugar.

The art originated in Champagne, where the best sparkling wines are produced, and whence it has spread to the Rhine, the Moselle, and other districts. A champagne which contains relatively little sugar is called "dry"; it is chiefly this kind which is imported into Great Britain, where champagne is used habitually principally as a dinner wine; in France a sweet wine is preferred. At the presentday wine is practically a European product, although a certain quantity is made in the United States, at the Cape of Good Hope, and in Australia.

France shows to-day, and has during several isolated seasons the past twenty years, shown herself to be the most remarkable wine-producing country country in the world's history, and this in face of the fact that the United States and Italy, with more territory suitable to grape-growing, and with wonderful natural advantages — and why? because she has taken advantage of her fitness of soil to the vine; her meteorological conditions; her geographical positions as regards the European markets, and incidentally those of the world, and partly to the aptitude of its inhabitants, that France developed the position which it now holds.

Spain is second only in reputation to France among wine-growing countries; its white wine, known as sherry, first brought it into prominence. Sherry, so called from the town of Jerez (Xeras) de la Frontera, the headquarters of this industry. There are several different varieties of sherry, which may be divided into the Amontillado and Manzanilla classes. The Amontillado class may again be divided into *fina* and *olloroso,* the former being the more delicate. The generous, full flavored wines known as Port, are the produce of the district of Alto Douro, in the northeast of Portugal, and thence shipped to and from Oporto.

Home Industry.

In our own country the cultivation of the vine has made rapid progress of late years, and American wines are steedily taking the place of the foreign product. The soil and climate of the Pacific Coast seem best adapted to the growth of the vine, and wine-making is very likely to become one of the leading industries of California. The Mission grape (being the first) is supposed to have been imported from Mexico by the Franciscan fathers about the year 1769. Subsequently varieties of French, German, and Spanish wines were introduced into the state. In Ohio upon the shores of Lake Erie and along the Ohio river the vine is extensively cultivated. The champagnes and clarets made in the neighborhood of Sandusky and Cleveland are produced in considerable quantities.

New York, Missouri, Illinois, and Pennsylvania are likewise large producing states, the largest wine manufacturing establishment being in New York State, Steuben County. The total annual production of wine in the United States now amounts to about 35,000,000 gallons.

Whiskey.

Whisky or whiskey, a spirit distilled fordrinking, which originated, at least so far as regards the name, with the Celtic inhabitants of Ireland and Scotland, and its manufacture and use still continues to be closely associated with those two countries.

Distilled spirit first became popularly known as aqua vitæ, and it was originally used only as a powerful medicinal agent. It was not till about the middle of the 17th century that it came into use in Scotland as an intoxicating beverage. It is only the finer qualities of matured malt and grain whiskey that can be used as simple or unblended spirit. In the United States whiskey is distilled chiefly from corn and rye, wheat and barley malt being used, though only to a limited extent. Whiskey is greatly improved by age; it is not mellow, nor its flavor agreeable until it is several years old. Whiskey seems to be the most favored drink in America for purposes of stimulation, and in uncertain moments when one is undecided as to what to take it is generally regarded by steady drinkers as the purest and most reliable drink. They appear to know good whiskey by the taste of it.

Brewing.

Is the art of preparing an exhilarating or intoxicating beverage by means of a process of fermentation. In the modern acceplation of the word, brewing is the operation of preparing beer and ales from any farinaceous grain, chiefly from barley, which is at first malted and ground, and its fermentable substance extracted by warm water. This infusion is evaporated by boiling, hops having been added to preserve it. The liquor is then fermented. The art was known and practiced by the Egyptians many hundred years before the Christian era, and afterward by the Greeks, Romans, and ancient Gauls, from whom it has been handed down to us. All countries, whether civilized or savage, have, in every age, prepared an intoxicating drink of some kind. Great care must be taken when buying for malting, for sometimes the grain is doctored by kiln-bleaching, or dried at too great a heat. Several samples, too, may be mixed, in which case they will not grow regularly, as heavier barley generally requires to be longer in steep; and the grains, broken by the drum of the threshing-machine being set too close, spoil a sample. Those cut into sections will not germinate, but in warm weather putrefy, as is evident from their blue-gray and moldy appearance and offensive smell while germinating. A good bayer will, by the use of a skillful hand, estimate very closely the weight per bushel in bulk. His eye will tell him if the grain has been cut before being ripe, in which case there will be a variety in the color of the barley-corns, some being bright and some a dead, grayish yellow. In consequence of being sown in spring, and not undergoing the equalizing tendency of winter, barley is, of all grain, the most liable to ripen in a patchy manner. and not come to perfection simultaneously. The buyer has also to judge if it has been heated, or "mow-burnt," while lying in the field after being cut, or in the stack.

DETROIT BREWING CO.,

Brewers of the Famous Brands

Bohemian, Erlanger, Absolutely Pure, Wholesome, and Delicious.

and **Export Beers.**

DETROIT, MICH.

Correspondence Solicited.

Health and Alcohol.

The British Medical Association, moved by the outcry against the use of alcoholic drinks, and wishing for some definite and reliable information as to the influence of alcohol on the duration of life, appointed a commission not long ago to gather statistics in the premises. The observations made included 4234 cases of deaths in five classes of individuals, and here are the results in the average age attained by each case: Total abstainers, 51 years and 1 month; moderate drinkers, 63 years and ½ month; occasional drinkers, 59 years and 2 months, habitual drinkers, 57 years and 2 months; drunkards, 53 years and ½ month. It appears that moderate drinkers live longer than anybody else, and total abstainers are the shortest lived.

BURNET HOUSE CINCINNATI

GEO. A. VANDEGRIFT,
Vice-President.

GEO. D. POTTS,
Treasurer.

THE BURNET HOUSE,

CINCINNATI, OHIO.

Most Centrally Located on Vine St., cor. Third, adjoining Chamber of Commerce.

The Palatial Hotel of the Queen City.

Convenient to all Places of Amusement. Wholesale and Retail Stores, Railroads, etc.

Electric Lighted Throughout.

Large Parlor on Office Floor, suitable for Conventions, Private Gatherings, etc. : : :

American Plan, $3.00 to $5.00 per Day.

J. W. DUNKLEE,
President and Manager.

RECIPES FOR COOKING

— BY —

JOSEPH MAESTRANI,

(CHEF BURNET HOUSE.)

Green Sea Turtle Soup.

(For 6 people.)

Place a pint of green turtle cut into pieces in a saucepan with two pints broth, add boquet, a glass of Madeira wine, a little red pepper, a tablespoonful salt, a little nutmeg, a teaspoonful English sauce, and the same of Espagnol sauce. Boil for 20 minutes, and serve with sliced lemon, after removing boquet.

Mock Turtle.

To be prepared as for green turtle, substituting a pint of cooked calf's head for the turtle.

Deviled Crabs.

(For 1 dozen.)

Take 1 quart crab meat, season salt, pepper, and nutmeg, tumbler Worcestershire sauce, put in pan, cook slowly, add a little cream sauce for thickening, cook half an hour, fill shells with preparation, mix a little mustard and Worcestershire, and cover it over outside, baking till brown.

How to Cook a Ham Properly.

Select a medium lean ham and steep in cold water during a whole night, place in saucepan, and cover it over with $\frac{2}{3}$ cider, $\frac{1}{3}$ water, boil for $2\frac{1}{2}$ hours, then take it out, trim nicely and remove upper skin and sprinkle 1 pound sugar over it and bake in oven till brown; serve either warm or cold, as preferred.

Clam Chowder.

(For 6 people.)

Prepare $\frac{1}{2}$ gallon boullion or stock, cut 3 onions fine, cut up $\frac{1}{2}$ pound salt pork in shape dice, put in pan the onions and pork, fry slowly, then put 5 dozen clams, with their own juice, all together in one pan, cut up 2 potatoes raw, cook slowly until potatoes are cooked, season with pepper, salt, and a little thime, skim off and serve.

Genuine English Plum Pudding.

One pound suet, ½ pound cracker meal, ½ pound flour, 1 pound raisins, 1 pound currants, 1 pound chopped citron, ¼ pound almonds, ½ ounce baking powder, ½ cup molasses, ½ teaspoonful cinnamon, little mace, 2 lemons (using rind and juice), 1 pound brown sugar, 1 glass brandy, 1 glass Madeira wine. Put in cloth and boil for three hours. Serve with hard or brandy sauce.

BY HARRY STAHL,

(CONFECTIONER BURNET HOUSE.)

New England Bread.

Take 7 pounds Gold Medal flour, 1 ounce compressed yeast, ¼ pound Indian meal, 1 ounce salt, 4 ounces butter, 2 ounces sugar; first scald meal with 1 quart boiling water; when cold, mix in all the other ingredients; add in milk sufficient to form a slack dough; be sure to mix well. Put in bread pans, let rise, and bake in medium-heated oven about 35 minutes.

Tea Biscuits.

Take 3 pounds Gold Medal flour, ½ pound butter, 3 ounces baking powder, 1 ounce salt; mix light with 1 quart sweet milk. Cut out and bake immediately.

Sweet Muffins.

(a la Lookout Mountain.)

¾ pound sugar, ½ pound butter, 10 eggs, 1¼ pounds Gold Medal flour, 1 pint milk, 1 ounce baking powder; work up butter and sugar to cream, then add eggs, milk, flour, and baking powder. Mix well, and divide into 30 muffin pans.

Cheese Sauce.

Melt one tablespoonful of butter and add same amount of flour; when smooth add one half pint milk and boil until thick and creamy; then add four tablespoonfuls of grated cheese (Parmesan the best) and pour over cauliflower.

July Dinner for Five Persons.

Bisque Soup.

Roast Chicken with Mushrooms.

New Potatoes.   Green Peas.

Compote Salad.

———

Frozen Custard.

———

Chicken to be split on back. buttered and roasted.

Cost —

Soup	25
Chicken, 4 lb at 18c	72c
Mushrooms	20c
Potatoes	10c
Peas	15c
Compote	20c
Salad	8c
	——— $ 1.45

Custard, 1 qt. milk, 6c; 4 eggs, 10c; vanilla andmsugar, 4c; ice, 15c . . 40

———

Total cost . . . . $ 2.10

Menu for July Dinner.

Fillets of Fish.   Sliced Cucumbers.

———

Roast Ribs of Beef.

Cauliflower with Cheese Sauce.

Boiled New Potatoes.

Beet Salad.

Cherry Sherbet.   Wafers.

Fillets of Fish.

Cut any fish into slices one inch thick, wash and wipe dry; sprinkle a platter with chopped onion, lay the fillets on top of this, and dust with salt and pepper. Mix three tablespoonfuls of olive oil and one of vinegar thoroughly and moisten the fish and stand aside one or two hours. When ready to cook dip the fillets first in egg, then in bread-crumbs, and fry in hot fat. Garnish with lettuce or cress and quarters of lemons.

Boiled Cauliflower.

Pick off the outer leaves, cut off the stem close to the bottom of the flowerets; wash in cold water; then soak with top downward in cold water for one hour. Tie it in a piece of cheese-cloth and put in salted boiling water, stem downward, and boil till tender. When done, remove carefully to dish and serve with cheese sauce.

Thanksgiving Dinner

BLUE POINTS.

♦

SALTED ALMONDS, with Cheese Sticks.

———

CREAM OF CAULIFLOWER. CONSOMME d'Orleans.

———

SMALL PATTIE, au Salpicon.

———

BOILED STRIPED BASS, Nonpareil.

Hollandaise   Potatoes.

CELERY.   SLICED TOMATOES.   CUCUMBERS.

———

TENDERLOIN OF BEEF, Larded, aux Cepes.

MASHED POTATOES.   ASPARAGUS, AU BEURRE.

ROAST SUCKLING PIG, with Baked Apples.

CANDIED SWEET POTATOES.   STRING BEANS.

YOUNG TURKEY, Chestnut Dressing, Cranberry Sauce.

BOILED ONIONS.   GREEN PEAS.

———

BAKED CHICKEN PIE, Family Style.

BRAISED SWEETBREADS, a la St Cloud.

♦

Champagne Punch.

SUGAR WAFERS.

♦

ROAST REDHEAD DUCK, au Cresson.

Mayonnaise of Lettuce.

———

PLUM PUDDING, Hard and Brandy Sauce.

MINCE PIE. GREEN APPLE PIE.   PUMPKIN PIE.

MARASCHINO JELLY. MERINGUED APRICOT TARTLETS.
FROZEN NESSELRODE PUDDING. ASSORTED CAKES.

NUTS and RAISINS. MINT DROPS. FRUIT. LAYER FIGS.

SWEET CRAB CIDER.

CHEESE.   COFFEE.   CRACKERS.

Burnet House,

THURSDAY, NOVEMBER 28, 1895.

LIQUORS TO SERVE WITH CERTAIN SPECIFIED FOODS.

Fashion, taste, and the instincts of the stomach, suggest the following:

Raw oysters — Sauterne, white Burgundies, or hock.

Soup — Sherry or Madeira.

Fish — Claret, Sauterne, or hock.

Roast (*relves*) — Burgundy or champagne, Roman or Kirsch punch.

Second course roast (game and poultry) — Old Champagnes, sparkling Moselles, clarets, red Burgundies, etc.

Entrees — Champagne.

Game and salads — Champagne.

Dessert — No liquors, or perhaps some fine Hungarian wine, or burnt brandy with black coffee.

With lunch in which cheese and rye or other bread, or cereal or starchy products predominate, the thing most used, and which most aids digestion, is beer, ale, porter, or stout.

Beer is not much drawn from the wood now, except in very small bars and at country crossroads. It is just as good drawn from the cellar through pipes plated inside with tin; but they must be kept scrupulously clean, and every morning three or four glasses of beer should be drawn off and thrown away. Pipes should be cleansed every week with a strong solution of sal soda and hot water.

THE MODEL BARTENDER.

He should be a man of good character, straight personal habits, good temper, cheerful, obliging, wide-awake, quick, graceful, attentive, sympathetic, yet too smart to be "worked," neither grum nor too talkative, of neat appearance and well dressed. He should study the tastes of the patrons. For instance, in mixing a cocktail most clerks make the mistake of putting in too mueh bitters, in which case the drink is spoiled, or rather, is unpalatable to the customer. Most men like but very little bitters. You should, in order to become proficient and popular, study all the points in the mixing of all drinks. There can be too much syrup or sugar, lemon juice or other ingredient used, in the same way as too much bitters in a cocktail. This is a profession that every man can not master. There are men who would not make a first-class bar clerk in a lifetime. A clerk should not encourage "hangers-on," loungers, or men under the influence of drink. In fact, he should never sell or give to a man in his cups, for this feature casts the greatest odium on our business, which could be made as legitimate as any if in the hands of proper persons.

PREPARATION FOR CUSTOMERS.

The first thing to be done in the morning upon opening a saloon is to look after ventilation. There is generally a very odious smell about a place that has been lightly closed during the night, and it is as unwholesome as it is disagreeable. It should be gotten rid of as soon as possible. See that you have enough fine ice prepared to serve your morning customers with drinks, and if the man on watch the night before has failed to fill his bottles, you must perform this duty at once, and place them on ice so that your customers may not have to use warm liquors. You must keep filling them up all day to supply the drain on them, and to avoid serving warm liquors. Polish up your glasses between drinks, and always be ready for customers. See to it that the place is neat and tidy; the window-panes, showcases and nickel-plating clear as crystal, and bright as new minted coins; the linen towels white as snow; the lunch fresh and inviting. A progressive clerk, and the proprietor too, for that matter, will visit other places to see what landable innovations are being made, what new inducements are being offered. Make your own domains correspondingly or surpassingly attractive, and give the boys a right royal welcome.

HINTS FOR YOUNG BARTENDERS.

1. An efficient bartender's first aim should be to please his customers, paying particular attention to meet the individual wishes of those whose tastes and desires he has already watched and ascertained; and, with those whose peculiarities he has had no opportunity of learning, he should politely inquire how they wish their beverage served, and use his best judgment in endeavoring to fill their desires to their entire satisfaction. In this way he will not fail to acquire popularity and success.

2. Ice must be washed clean before being used, and then never touched with the hand, but placed in the glass either with an ice-scoop or tongs.

3. Fancy drinks are usually ornamented with such fruits as are in season. When a beverage requires to be strained into a glass, the fruit is added after straining; but when this is not the case, the fruit is introduced into the glass at once. Fruit, of course, must not be handled, but picked with a silver spoon or fork.

4. In preparing any kind of a hot drink, the glass should always be first rinsed rapidly with hot water: if this is not done the drink can not be

served sufficiently hot to suit a fastidious customer. Besides, the heating of the glass will prevent it from breaking when the boiling water is suddenly introduced.

5. In preparing cold drinks great discrimination should be observed in the use of ice. As a general rule, shaved ice should be used when spirits form the principal ingredient of the drink, and no water is employed. When eggs, milk, wine, vermouth, Seltzer or other mineral waters are used in preparing a drink, it is better to use small lumps of ice, and these should always be removed from the glass before serving to the customer.

6. Sugar does not readily dissolve in spirits; therefore, when making any kind of hot drink, put sufficient boiling water in the glass to dissolve the sugar, before you add the spirits.

7. When making cold mixed drinks it is usually better to dissolve the sugar with a little cold water, before adding the spirits. This is not, however, necessary when a quantity of shaved ice is used. In making cocktails the use of syrup has almost entirely superseded white sugar.

8. When drinks are made with eggs, or milk, or both, and hot wine or spirits is to be mixed with them, *the latter must always be poured on the former gradually,* and the mixture stirred briskly during the process; otherwise the eggs and milk will curdle. This is more particularly the case when large quantities of such mixtures are to be prepared. Such drinks as "English Rum Flip," "Hot Eggnog" and "Mulled Wine" are sure to be spoiled unless these precautions are observed.

DON'TS FOR YOUNG BARTENDERS.

Don't bring yourself into prominence before a crowd at the bar. Be polite and approachable, but let them advance to you.

Don't join in any conversation, but if it is general you may seem interested.

Don't volunteer any opinions unless your patrons express a desire, or at least a willingness to hear you.

Don't express your sentiments at all if at variance with the majority, unless very important interests are at stake.

Don't be too positive about things. You may be in error.

Don't look fiercely at people, or talk loud and harshly, but cultivate a smiling countenance and quiet, but firm tone of speech.

Don't occupy too much space, but give your colleagues behind the bar a chance.

Don't fail to put things in their places, so that you and your coworkers will know where they are when you want them.

Don't fail to get pay for all drinks.

Don't be in too great a hurry to find out what a party of gentlemen want as they approach the bar.

Don't let them feel that you begrudge the space they occupy while they talk. Sometimes placing glasses of water before them will break the ice on the subject.

Don't use a wet glass if there is a dry one to be had.

Don't forget to serve your effervescent drinks last in waiting ou a party.

Jos. J. Ciarlo,

Photographer

210 & 212 W. 4th St.,
Bet. Elm and Plum Sts.,
CINCINNATI, O.

514 York Street,
NEWPORT, KY.

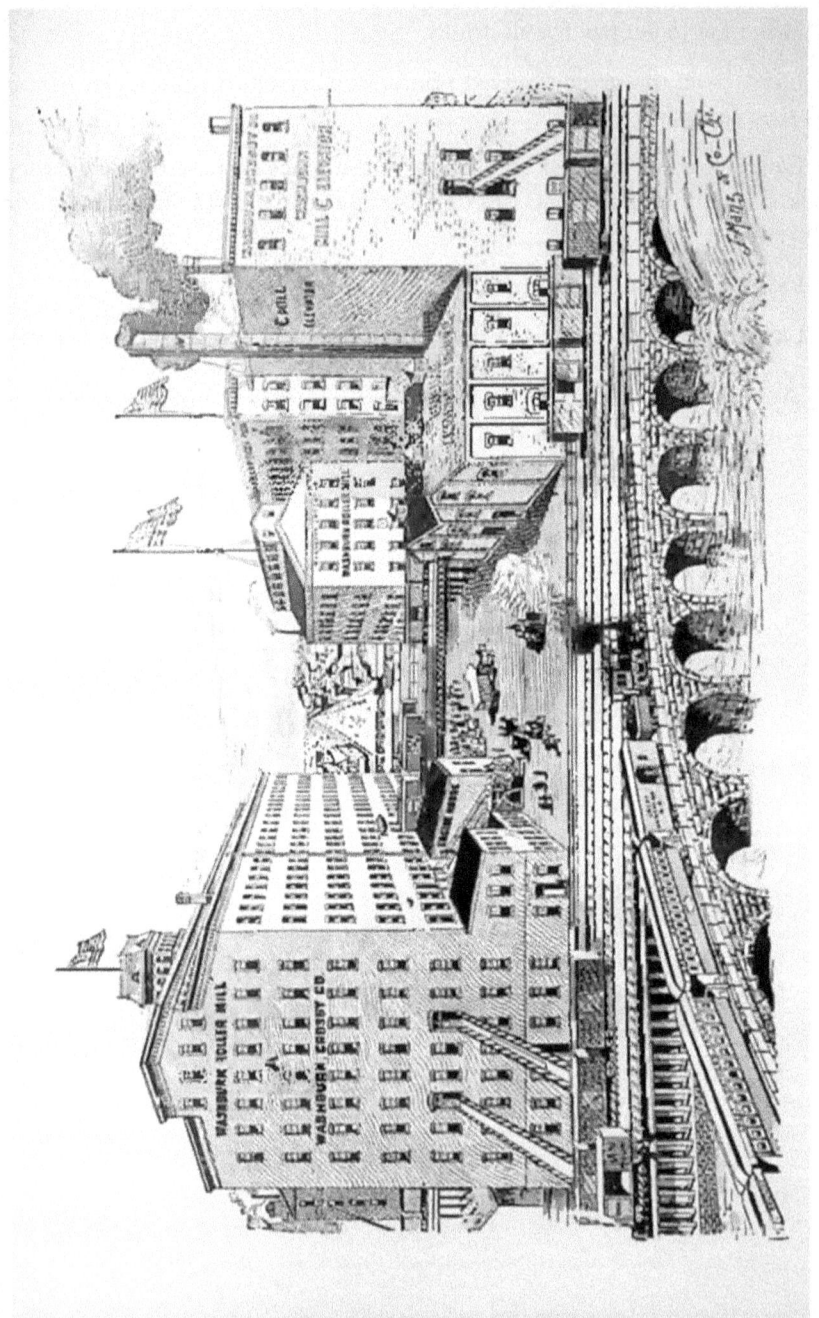

WASHBURN, CROSBY'S FLOUR

Took First Prize at the

Centennial Exhibition in Philadelphia, 1876,

at—

Millers' Exhibition at Cincinnati, 1880,

at—

World's Fair, Chicago, 1893.

500 barrels of Flour are made daily by the Washburn Crosby Co. Mills. For sale by all first-class Grocers in America.

HEID & KOSS, Sole Agents,
Burnet House Block,   CINCINNATI, O.

Telephone 473.

ESTABLISHED 1840.

The Joseph R. Peebles' Sons Co.

JOSEPH S. PEEBLES, PRES'T.

GROCERS, WINE MERCHANTS,

AND IMPORTERS OF HAVANA CIGARS.

Agents for the famous "EL PRINCIPE DE GALES" CIGARS for twenty-five years. Nothing finer made.

Largest Handlers of Pure, Ripe, Old, Mellow **WHISKIES** In the United States.

———— SPECIALTIES ————

Cased Whiskies
- JAS. E. PEPPER, 1840 BRAND.
- PEEBLES "SWEET HICKORY."
- PEEBLES "OLD CABINET" WHISKY.
- MELLWOOD BOURBON.
- NORMANDY RYE.
- LIVE OAK RYE.

We are the Distillers' Authorized Bottlers of Mellwood and Normandy Whiskies.

Distributors of Hiram Walker & Sons' Celebrated "CANADIAN CLUB" Whisky.

With each case of **PEEBLES' "OLD CABINET"** we furnish gratis 12 "Old Nick" Corkscrews, which retail for 50 Cents each, and with five cases we furnish the handsomest picture ever seen by the whisky trade. It is lithographed on glass in eighteen colors. Hotel Supplies a Specialty. Write for Trade Price-List.

CINCINNATI, OHIO.

P. S.—PEEBLES claim to be the Largest Distributors of PURE FOOD PRODUCTS in the Ohio Valley, and carry in stock every article used in a first-class bar.

BURDICK'S CAFÉ,

FOR LADIES AND GENTLEMEN.

PRIVATE DINING-ROOM
FOR PARTIES.

Live Lobsters, Shell Oysters, Clams, Fish, and Game in Season.

TELEPHONE 938.

Nos. 9 & 11 West Fifth St.

Central Saloon

LEW KRAFT, Proprietor.

S. W. Cor. Carlisle and Central Avenues,

CINCINNATI.

FINE WHISKIES.

CHOICE WINES,
LIQUORS,
AND CIGARS
 A SPECIALTY.

ESTABLISHED 1855.

J. McArdle,

IMPORTER AND TAILOR,

GRAND OPERA-HOUSE BLOCK,

CINCINNATI.

J. H. RICHTER,

Maker of Fine Clothing,

Nos. 221 & 223 WEST FIFTH STREET

Corner Home Street.

ESTABLISHED 1855.

All Kinds of Mixed Drinks.

J. J. TIERNEY,

SALOON,

S. W. Cor. Fifth and Central Ave.,

CINCINNATI, O.

Oscar and James E. Pepper
WHISKIES
A Specialty.

LOCAL AND LONG-DISTANCE TELEPHONE, 7832

The Jung Brewing Co.

BREWERS AND BOTTLERS OF

FINE BEERS.

Absolutely Pure, Wholesome, and Nutritious.

FREEMAN AVE.
From Garden to Bank Street,
CINCINNATI, O.

H. WM. MEIER,

Successor to GOBRECHT & MEIER.

Wholesale Liquors,

WINES, AND BRANDIES.

122 W. Court Street, Cincinnati, O.

Telephone 204.

Sole Agent for "Almanaris Natural Mineral Water."

Importer of RHINE WINES.

THEODORE GROSS
The Home
15 W. 6TH ST
Cincinnati, O.

FINE LIQUORS AND CIGARS.

Dinner Lunch 11—2.

ASK YOUR GROCER FOR

"Banner Brand"
Hams and Breakfast Bacon

Insist on getting The Banners. They are the Best.

The BANNER PACKING & PROVISION CO.

N. W. Corner Bank and Patterson Streets,

CINCINNATI, OHIO.

 ## "Big Four"

BEST LINE TO
NEW YORK AND BOSTON

"Southwestern Limited"—"Knickerbocker Special"
"Finest Trains in America."

WAGNER BUFFET SLEEPING CARS, COMBINATION, LIBRARY, SMOKING, AND
CAFE CARS, MODERN COACHES AND DINING CARS.

NO FERRY AT NEW YORK.

St. Louis:
No Tunnel!
No Smoke!

Chicago:
Best Terminal Station!

Cincinnati:
Central Union Station!

E. O. McCormick,
Passenger Traffic Manager.

D. B. Martin,
Gen'l Pass'r & Ticket Agt.

WELLMAN'S

Money-Savers' Specials . . .

TRY ONE OF OUR EXTRA FINE, FULL-CONCAVE, FINELY TEMPERED RAZORS FROM THE BEST STEEL. MAILED TO ANY ADDRESS. **$1.50**

SAWS!

Panel, $1.00.   Hand, $1.25.   Rip, $1.25.
LONDON SPRING SKEW BACK WARRANTED.

A 32 OR 38-CALIBER, DOUBLE-ACTING, SELF-EJECTING REVOLVER, S. & W. PATTERN, $3.50. CARTRIDGES 50c. A BOX.

A FULL LINE OF

HARDWARE, CUTLERY AND MECHANIC'S TOOLS

AT LOW PRICES.

A. F. WELLMAN,

6th and Main Streets,   CINCINNATI, OHIO.

SEND FOR CIRCULAR OF WELLMAN'S CELEBRATED RHEUMATISM CURE. HUNDREDS CURED BY THIS CURE. PRICE $1.00.

HALL'S
DRUG STORES.

For Everything in the Drug Line.

SODA WATER.	SODA WATER.
4th and Elm.	4th and Walnut.

4th and ELM, Phone 760.   4th and WALNUT, Phone 582.

Parties at a distance requiring any number of copies of this book will address

C. F. LAWLOR,

Burnet House.   Cincinnati, Ohio.

Oskamp, Nolting & Co.

MANUFACTURERS AND DEALERS IN

FIRST-CLASS BAR APPURTENANCES,

Wine Coolers, Ice Tubs, Bar Pitchers, Julep Strainers, Bar Spoons, Sugar Sifters, Etc.

IF YOU THINK OF BUYING A

DIAMOND, WATCH, CLOCK,

OR PIECE OF

FINE JEWELRY, SILVERWARE, ETC.

Write for our "BLUE BOOK." It will give you new ideas and illustrations of over 2,000 fine articles suitable for presents or your own use.

OSKAMP, NOLTING & CO.,
WHOLESALE AND RETAIL JEWELERS,
5th and Vine Streets,
CINCINNATI, O.

OPENING WINES.

In opening still wines the top of the capsule should be cut, leaving the shining metal below to form an ornamental band. Wipe off the top with a napkin, and, if you serve it, pour with the right hand, holding the bottle in the center of the bulge, pressing lightly with the thumb and fingers. This is more graceful than grasping it impetuously by the neck. It is a custom, more in America than elsewhere, for gentlemen to pour out their own liquors, especially if in a party.

In opening Champagne and other effervescent drinks, including malt liquors, cut the band below the cork with the nippers, and the wires will come off easily by a twist of the hand. It will be necessary to use the corkscrew in case of malt liquors not confined by the patent rubber cork, and there is great danger of cutting the left hand in case of breakage, if, as is generally the case, the bottle is grasped by the neck. It should be held firmly with the left hand near the bottom of the bulge, and the cork should be drawn steadily with the right, and without shaking the bottle. There is no danger by this method.

To Serve Champagne.

Place the required number of Champagne glasses on the bar filled with fine ice; take wine carefully from the ice and place on bar; remove the wire from the cork with nippers; if corded, be sure and cut all clean from neck of bottle and cork; while doing this do not remove the bottle from the bar; when done, pull the cork about one third out, wipe the lip of the bottle carefully with a clean napkin or towel, throw the ice from the champagne glasses and draw the cork slowly; pour a little wine in each glass, then commence again with the first and pour as much as you can without having the foam run over the sides; continue this until all the glasses are filled. Always leave the bottle on the bar with the cork by its side or on the top of the bottle until the entire party have finished their wine.

To Frappe Champagne.

Place the bottle in the champagne pail, fill with fine ice and salt; whirl or twist the bottle several times, and it will become almost frozen.

CORDIALS.

Kirschwasser, a spirit from black cherries, in great demand throughout Europe, is becoming abundant in the United States, and equal to any in Europe. Kirsch is an excellent digestive and tonic for throat, lungs and entire system; used in sorbets, etc. A punek of kirsch, coffee, sugar and ice-water makes a delicious drink in warm weather.

Benedictine, distilled at Fecamp, Normandy, is a very famous old cordial, originally prepared exclusively by the Benedictine monks, but since the French Revolution it has been made by a secular company. It is known principally as a genitial stimulant.

Chartreuse is a tonic cordial, very palatable, and highly esteemed for its stomachic and antifebrile virtues. It is prepared by the distillation of various aromatic plants, especially nettles, growing in the Alps, carnations, absinthium, and the young buds of the pine tree. There are three kinds, green, yellow, and white.

Maraschino originated with the Italians. For years the Pope sent this delicious liquor to all the grandees of the world. Queen Elizabeth of England was extravagantly fond of it, and, as if to honor it, drank it from a goblet of gold. The basis of Maraschino is black cherries, jasmine, roses, orange flowers, etc., fermented and distilled. It is recommended as an anodyne against nervousness. It is extensively used in the preparation of jellies, sorbets, pastry, etc.

Montana is prepared from the juices of plants, flowers, roots, etc., growing on the highest mountains of America, principally the Rockies and Alleghanies. It is a powerful digestive, suitable for everybody, but principally for the aged and debilitated. It should generally be taken after dinuer.

Curaçao, dub (sweet) and sec (dry), also triple sec, has for its basis the peel of the young bitter orange growing generally in the island of Curaçao, a possession of Holland, off South America. It is a digestive, and is used as a preventive against fever. It is white or green in color.

Anisette is recommended for the cure of flatulency, colic, etc. The aroma and flavor of this delicious, ancient, and popular liquor is obtained from annis seed.

Absinthe (green or white), a bitter beverage used as an appetizer, and bitterly denounced and as warmly praised by different *critiques* the past century. The present method of preparation dates back only sixty years. Formally it was sirnply an infusion of herbs in white wine. In Normandy and in certain countries around the Alps it is still prepared in that crude way. The distillers of Besançon, Pontarlier, and Couvet hit on the idea of distilling the Absinthe herb (wormwood), adding annis, fennel, and corriander seeds, etc., *ad lib.*, these making an agreeable beverage. Absinthe so made soon had considerable success, which had the usual effect of bringing out the injurious trash made from oils, essences, etc.

Absinthe, if properly made, is healthful — a wonderful appetizer and soother of the nerves — if not taken in excess. It is usually taken with half a glass of water to a small wineglass of Absinthe. The water is allowed to drip on the Absinthe so as to milk or pearl it. Taken pure it has the same properties as peppermint in cases of colic or cramps. To some tastes a cocktail is much improved by the addition of two or three drops of Absinthe.

SYRUPS, ESSENCES, TINCTURES, ETC.

These preparations consist of ingredients used in the following recipes for making prepared punches, cocktails, etc.

Plain Syrup.

Take 6½ pounds of loaf-sugar.

½ gallon of water.

The white of 1 egg.

Boil until dissolved, and filter through flannel.

Gum Syrup.

Take 14 pounds of loaf-sugar.

1 gallon of water.

Boil together for five minutes, and add water to make up to 2 gallons.

Lemon Syrup.

Take 5 gallons of gum syrup.

4 ounces of tartaric acid.

1 ounce of oil of lemon.

1 pint of alcohol.

Cut the oil of lemon in the alcohol, add the tartaric acid, and mix thoroughly with the syrup.

Essence of Lemon.

Take 1 ounce of oil of lemon.

1 quart of alcohol (95 per cent).

½ pint of water.

1½ ounces of citric acid.

Tincture of Orange Peel.

Take 1 pound of dried orange peel (ground).

1 gallon of spirits (95 percent).

Place them in a closely corked vessel for ten days; strain and bottle for use.

Tincture of Lemon Peel.

Cut into small chips the peel of twelve large lemons; place it in a glass jar, and pour over it one gallon spirits seventy percent; let it stand until the lemon peel has all sunk to the bottom of the liquor; it is then ready for use without either filtering or straining.

Tincture of Cloves.

Take one pound of ground cloves; warm them over a fire until quite hot; put them quickly into a jar, pour on them one gallon ninety-five percent alcohol; cover them air-tight, and let them stand for ten days; draw off into bottles and cork close.

Tincture of Cinnamon.

Place two pounds of ground cinnamon into a jar, with one gallon ninety-five percent alcohol, closely covered; at the end of eight days strain the liquor clear; wash the sediment with one quart proof spirits; strain it; mix the two liquors together, and filter through blotting paper.

Rollman & Sons,

General Dry Goods, Cloaks, Millinery, and Fine Shoes.

6, 8, 10, 12, 14 and 16 West Fifth Street, near Vine,

CINCINNATI, O.

The Cuvier

CHAS. CRAMER,
N.W. Cor. 4th & Central Ave.
CINCINNATI, O.

Frohman, Mgr.

THE

Merchants' Cafe

No. 61 MAIN STREET,

CINCINNATI, O.

Old Whiskies
Hauck's Beer.

JAS. QUATMAN,
PROPRIETOR.

Telephone 5.

TURPIN GERARD,

CIGARS

35 Fountain Square,

JOHNSTON BUILDING,   CINCINNATI.

Distributing Agent
"LA DUCHESSE"
5-Cent Cigar.

Anheuser-Busch Brewing Association.

CELEBRATED BUDWEISER AND LAGER BEER.

CINCINNATI BRANCH, 324 Main Street.

JOHN PFITZENREITER, Mgr.

J. F. FLOCKEN,

PROPRIETOR OF

"The Lodge,"

No. 205 (Old) Walnut Street,

(New Number, 513.)

OPPOSITE POST-OFFICE,

CINCINNATI, - OHIO.

Handsomely Furnished Rooms for Gentlemen.

CHAS. ULMER & CO.,

Merchant Tailors

No. 227 E. PEARL STREET, New Number.

No. 27 East Pearl Street, Old Number.

CINCINNATI, O.

Wm. L. Theis & Co.

HATTERS

S. W. Corner Fifth and Main Streets,

CINCINNATI, O.

YOUNG

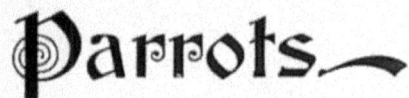 WARRANTED TO LEARN TO TALK.

$5.00 EACH.

THE ESPICH BIRD STORE,
15 East 6th St., bet. Vine and Walnut Streets,
CINCINNATI, OHIO.

HEADQUARTERS FOR
Dogs, Monkeys, Goldfish, and Pets of all Kinds.

Light, Clean, Well-Ventilated Rooms.
Rooms, 35, 50 and 75 Cents per Day.
Liberal Reduction by Week or Month.

Hotel Lamar,
ROOMS ONLY.

S. E. Cor. Sixth and Elm Streets,

CINCINNATI, OHIO.

3 SQUARES FROM FOUNTAIN.
3 SQUARES FROM CITY HALL.

W. L. MOCKBEE,
MANAGER.

..DENTISTRY..

Teeth=$3 to $15

CROWN AND BRIDGEWORK
REASONABLE.

E. L. Nichols,

DENTIST.

OFFICE AND RESIDENCE:

Hotel Lamar, 147 West 6th Street,
CINCINNATI, OHIO.

OFFICE OPEN SUNDAYS AND EVENINGS.

... The ...

F. W. Cook Brewing Co.

EVANSVILLE, IND.

BREWERS
AND BOTTLERS OF

Absolutely Pure

BEER BARLEY, MALT AND HOPS.

Correspondence Solicited.

RICHARD MURPHY,

• PLUMBER •

COLUMBIA BUILDING,
113 West Seventh Street, 121 W. Seventh Street, (Old Number)
CINCINNATI, O.

TELEPHONE 1255.

HIGH-GRADE PLUMBING A SPECIALTY.

Jobbing promptly and properly attended to.
Estimates on all kinds of Plumbing cheerfully furnished.

THE FRENCH BROS. DAIRY CO.

PRODUCERS OF

PURE MILK AND CREAM.

FINE TABLE BUTTER
A SPECIALTY.

316 & 318 W. SEVENTH STREET.

W. T. WAGNER'S SONS

BOTTLERS OF

Selters,

Vichy,

Club Soda,

AND

IMPERIAL MINERAL WATER,

Prepared from Absolutely Pure Distilled Water.

712 RACE STREET,

Telephone 1602.   CINCINNATI, O.

ANDERSON BROS.,

DEALERS IN ALL KINDS OF

FRESH FISH, FROGS, TURTLES, SHRIMPS, LOBSTERS, SOFT-SHELL CRABS, ETC.

◄ IN SEASON. ►

140 W. SIXTH STREET.
TELEPHONE 1206.

John Schneider's Son & Co.,
FLOUR MILLS & BAKERY,

ALSO DEALERS IN
FLOUR, BRAN, RYE, SHORTS, AND MIDDLINGS.

Rye Flour and Rye Bread a Specialty.

1424-1426 WALNUT STREET,
Old No. 526 and 528 Walnut Street.

1419-1425 CLAY STREET,
Old No. 155, 157 and 159 Clay Street.

Cash Paid for Rye and Wheat. **CINCINNATI, O.**

BARBER SHOP,

9 & 11 W. Fourth St.

MITCHELL BUILDING,

Next Door to Chamber of Commerce.

SHAVING, 10 CENTS

J. F. HESSE, Prop.

J. F. HESSE, Prop.
J. R. HESSE, Manager.

GERDES HOTEL
BARBER SHOP
AND
BATH-ROOMS,

205 FIFTH STREET,

Between Plum and Elm Streets.

BATHS, 20 Cents.

JACOB FOX.   G. WM. FOX.

PIONEER UMBRELLA STORE.
ESTABLISHED 1845.

J. FOX & SON,

MANUFACTURERS,
WHOLESALERS AND RETAILERS OF

UMBRELLAS AND WALKING CANES

ORIGINAL RATTAN IN ALL SIZES

No. 419 Main Street, bet. Fourth and Fifth Sts.,

REPAIRING PROMPTLY AND NEATLY DONE.   **CINCINNATI, O.**

The Cincinnati Oyster & Fish Co.,

WHOLESALE AND RETAIL DEALERS IN

OYSTERS,
Fish, Game, Celery, etc.

35 W. Sixth St., Cincinnati, O.

TELEPHONE 259.   STEPHEN CHASE, SUPT.

BRANCHES:
THE CHASE-DAVIDSON CO., LOUISVILLE, KY.
CHASE & CO., CHATTANOOGA, TENN.
CHASE & CO., BALTIMORE, MD.

D. J. LEAHY & CO.

CIGAR MANUFACTURERS,

Office, Room D, Mitchell Bldg.

CINCINNATI, OHIO.

"OUR LEADERS," | "EL MANTOU,"
Re-Imported | All Havana
5 cent Cigars | 10 cent Cigars

M. S. GLENN,

Jas. E. Pepper Whiskey a Specialty.

GROCER,
TEA, WINE, AND
SPIRIT MERCHANT.

No. 744 W. THIRD STREET,
Old Number, 460 W. Third Street.

CINCINNATI, O.

Established 1852.

Stetter & Mangold,

Importers and Wholesale Dealers in

Foreign Wines & Liquors.

Large assortment of California Wines.
Family Trade a Specialty.

336 W. Sixth Street, - Cincinnati, O.
Old Number 254.

VOLZ'S

Open Day and Night.

San Francisco Bakery and Lunch Rooms.

BILL OF FARE consists of everything usually found in a first-class place. All kinds of meats, etc., to order. Roasts at noon. Oysters received daily in season.

TWO LARGE DINING-ROOMS.

75 & 77 W. Sixth St., - CINCINNATI, O.

S. N. MAXWELL,

Attorney at Law,

ST. PAUL BUILDING,

TELEPHONE 790.

CINCINNATI, O.

Write for prices on all kinds Slot Machines.
NAT. SLOT MACHINE COMPANY,
511 Vine St.,
Cincinnati, O.

FRANK OTTING,
Cigarist.

ALL KINDS OF
SMOKER'S ARTICLES,
511 Vine St., Cincinnati, O.

JAMES H. GRAHAM,
LEXINGTON PIKE DAIRY.

BUTTERMILK

Supplied to

Hotels, Restaurants, Saloons, Etc.

Address care of

C. H. BURDICK, Cincinnati, or

ERLANGER P. O., - - - - Kenton Co., Ky.

HERMAN WESSEL,

MANUFACTURER OF

❖ Mattresses and Bedding ❖

BLANKETS AND COMFORTS.

※ | COTS A SPECIALTY.

FEATHERS | FEATHERS RENOVATED
— BY —
※ | COLD-BLAST MACHINE.

Nos. 13 and 15 East Fifth Street, Fountain Square,
CINCINNATI, OHIO.

TELEPHONE 2198.

BACK BAY HOTELS,
BOSTON.

THE BRUNSWICK,
Boylston and Clarendon Streets, opposite Trinity Church and Massachusetts Institute of Technology. American and European Plan.

BARNES & DUNKLEE.

THE VENDOME,
Commonwealth Avenue and Dartmouth Street. American Plan exclusively.

C. H. GREENLEAF & CO.

AMOS BARNES.
JOHN W. DUNKLEE.
C. H. GREENLEAF

THE ORIENTAL,
DALLAS, TEXAS.

This elegant hotel has the largest and most luxuriously appointed rooms of any hotel in the State. Southern and eastern exposure. In the business part of the city. Convenient to postoffice, railroad stations, and churches. No better table in the South. Service of the best. A favorite with the tourist and traveling public. For circular, address W. J. ALDEN, Manager and Secretary, formerly of Vendome, Boston.

Gentlemen's.   Ladies'.

McGrath & Co.

Formerly COWEN & McGRATH,

DEALERS IN

Fine Footwear,

150 West Fifth St., bet. Race and Elm,
New Number, 116 West Fifth St.,

CINCINNATI, O.

Misses'.   Children's.

H. J. CAIN,

Dealer in and Shipper of

OYSTERS, FISH, GAME,

POULTRY, CELERY, FRUITS, AND VEGETABLES,

103 W. FIFTH ST., CINCINNATI, O.
BETWEEN VINE AND RACE STS.

Sole Agent for my own brand of Baltimore Oysters.

H. W. Moran Bros.

Fine Sugar-Cured Corned Beef,

112 W. Sixth Street, near Race,

CINCINNATI, O.

Hotels and Restaurants supplied. Choice Meats delivered, cooked, to Bar trade.
Handlers of Choice Meats only.

A. G. BUBBE,

DRUGGIST,

Successor to
J. C. Buttemiller,

S.E. Cor. Fifth & Mill Sts.,

CINCINNATI, O.

PRESCRIPTION PHARMACY.

COFFIN & WERLE,

AGENTS,

HEADQUARTERS FOR

Men's Neckwear, Collars, Cuffs

HANDKERCHIEFS,

SUSPENDERS AND UNDERWEAR.

SHIRTS MADE TO FIT
A SPECIALTY.

202 West Fifth St., CINCINNATI, O.

Second Door West of Elm.

MARTIN BURKE,

MANUFACTURER OF

MARBLE AND GRANITE

MONUMENTS,

657 W. FIFTH ST., bet. Mound and Park Sts.,

Large Stock
Always on Hand.   CINCINNATI, O.

HENRY TONJES,

Manufacturer of and Dealer In

FINE CIGARS
 - AND -
TOBACCOS.

710 W. FIFTH ST., bet. Park and Stone,

Box Trade a Specialty.   CINCINNATI, O.

THE
Snow Flake Laundry Co.

BRANCHES ALL OVER CITY AND SUBURBS.

OFFICE AND WORKS:

New No. 1218 & 1220 Race St.
Old No. 444 & 446 Race St.

CINCINNATI, OHIO.

Telephone 833.

Strictly First-Class Work Guaranteed.

GOODS CALLED FOR AND DELIVERED.

C. B. FISHBURN,
President.

J. GEO. ENGEL,
Sec'y and Treasurer.

THE GEO. WIEDEMANN BREWING CO.

Brewers of High-Grade Beers,

NEWPORT, KY.

COLUMBUS BRANCH

The Geo. Wiedemann Brew. Co.

M. Theado & Co.

AGENTS,

234 & 238 S. Fourth St., Columbus, O.

High-Grade Beers, in kegs and bottles, delivered to all parts of the city.
Finest Table Beer in the market.

TEL. 750.

CHAS. H. WUST & CO.

KNIT JACKETS,
UNDERWEAR,
AND
YARNS.

Manufacturers of and Dealers in

HOSIERY.

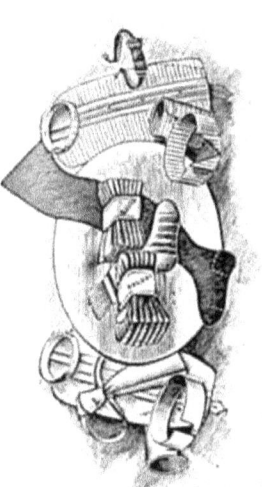

MEN'S FURNISHERS.

Stage, Base-Ball, and Bicycle Hosiery a Specialty.

228 Walnut Street, bet. 5th and 6th, Cincinnati, O.

New Number, 526 Walnut Street.

SUBURBAN DELIVERY DAILY.		SHAD. SHRIMP. SOFT CRABS.
WALNUT HILLS. AVONDALE. MT. AUBURN. CLIFTON.		CRAWFISH. TURTLES. FROGS.

Monday, 9 a. m. and 1 p. m.	
Tuesday, 9 " " 1 "	
Wednesday, 9 " " 1 "	**CHAS H. KEITH,**
Thursday, 9 " " 1 "	Wholesale and Retail Dealer in
Friday, 8 " " 1 "	
Saturday, 9 " " 1 "	
Sunday, 9 " " 1 "	

Oysters, Fish and Game

RED SNAPPERS A SPECIALTY.

New No. 554-556-558 West Sixth St.
Old No. 356-358-360 West Sixth St.   *Telephone 7032.*

E. D. SHAYS, AGENT,

DEALER IN FINE

HAVANA AND KEY WEST

Cigars and Tobacco

307 WEST FOURTH STREET.

Next to Gas Office,   **CINCINNATI.**

C. T. BENNETT.
A. A. JECKEL.

DRY CLEANING
A SPECIALTY.

PARISIAN DYE HOUSE,

RENOVATORS OF

Ladies' and Gents' Clothing

CLOTHING MADE TO ORDER.

107 East Sixth Street, CINCINNATI, OHIO.

Four Doors East of Walnut Street.

REPAIRING AND ALTERING ON SHORT NOTICE.

ARMOUR PACKING COMPANY.

(KANSAS CITY, MO.)

BRANCH HOUSE, Cincinnati, Ohio.

PACKERS
AND JOBBERS.

Beef and Provisions.

SPECIALTIES: White Label Soups & Helmet Canned Meats.

C. ROCKEL, Manager,

Telephone 365. 33 & 35 Main Street.

CHOICE WESTERN BEEF, VEAL, AND MUTTON OUR SPECIALTY.

FISCHER
STEEL RANGES.
"AMERICA'S BEST."

PLENTY HOT WATER FOR BATHS GUARANTEED

STOVE REPAIRS OF ALL KINDS THROUGHOUT.

The William G. Fischer Manufacturing Co.,
No. 9-19 CHURCH PLACE,
SOUTH OF POSTOFFICE, BET. FOURTH & FIFTH.

TELEPHONE *546. CINCINNATI, O.

THE MOST RELIABLE BRANDS OF HAVANA
CIGARS ON MARKET.

National Bouquets
AND El Mas Noble
MADE BY

P. F. CARCABA & CO.

H. L. KIRSTEIN, Sole Agent,

Telephone 5094.   2513 VINE STREET, Cor. Calhoun.

THE JOHN VAN RANGE CO.

KITCHEN OUTFITS
FOR HOTELS AND PUBLIC INSTITUTIONS.

)t-Water Urns, Chafing Dishes, Bar Utensils, etc.

NEW No. 419 ELM STREET,
OLD No. 169 ELM STREET,

4-6-8-10 CINCINNATI, O.
)ME STREET,

Meader's

44 East Fourth Street,
CINCINNATI.

For Cheap and Reliable R. R. Tickets.

JNO. P. LLOYD, Mgr.

ESTABLISHED OVER 35 YEARS.

WELLS' DRUG STORE.

EVERYTHING IN STOCK.

N. E. Cor. Fourth and Central Avenue,

TELEPHONE 1446. CINCINNATI.

GUS. BUNJES,

No. 1 MEAT STORE.

ALL KINDS OF

FRESH AND SALT MEATS,

SAUSAGES, ETC.

737 West Fourth Street, Between Mill and Stone.

J. C. GROENE & CO.,

SHEET MUSIC,
MUSICAL INSTRUMENTS,

No. 19 Arcade,   =   =   CINCINNATI, O.

SPECIALTIES:
Washburn Guitars,
Washburn Mandolins,
Fairbanks & Cole Banjos,
Band and Orchestra Music.

W. W. FRANKLIN,

Architect,

Rooms 24 and 26 Glenn Building,

S. W. Cor. Fifth and Race Sts.,   CINCINNATI, O.

F. G. CRAIG,

MANUFACTURER OF

———— OLD FASHION ————

SOUR MASH WHISKEY,

BERRY, HARRISON COUNTY, KY.

SCHMITTAUER'S

Prescription ✽ Pharmacy,

N. W. Cor. Sixth and York Streets,

Telephone 2263.   NEWPORT, KY.

Telephone 1501.   —THE—   Henry Verhage, Pres't.

CINCINNATI SODA WATER AND GINGER ALE CO.,

MANUFACTURERS OF

National Belfast Ginger Ale,

AND ALL KINDS OF

Soda and Mineral Waters.

1015 and 1017 Broadway. - - **CINCINNATI, O.**

Charging of Fountains a Specialty.

JOS. HARTMANN & SON,

Fashionable Tailors.

REASONABLE PRICES.

409 York Street,   -   NEWPORT, KY.

ESTABLISHED 1885.

KENTUCKY LAUNDRY,

W. A. PATERSON, Proprietor.

OFFICE AND WORKS:
636 Monmouth Street,
NEWPORT, KY.

LACKMAN'S
OLD LAGER
ON TAP.

JOHN C. HURLBRINK,

IMPORTED & DOMESTIC

Wines and Liquors,

S. W. Corner Carlisle Ave. and Mound St.,

CINCINNATI, O.

THE CARLISLE BUILDING & LOAN CO. MEETS MONDAY EVENINGS.

DAN. MURPHY,

Fine Old Whiskies,

WINES, AND CIGARS,

176 Vine St., CINCINNATI, O.

New Number, 424 Vine St.,   Between Fourth and Fifth.

ESTABLISHED 1868.

BRAMSCHE & KRENNING,

IMPORTERS AND WHOLESALE

LIQUOR DEALERS,

No. 32 Main Street,

CINCINNATI, OHIO.

Standard Bottling Works,

MANUFACTURERS OF ALL KINDS OF

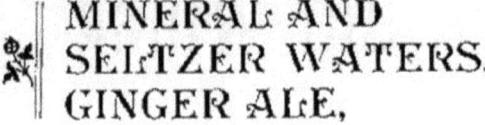

MINERAL AND SELTZER WATERS, GINGER ALE,

AND

The New Trilby Soda.

ALL ORDERS PROMPTLY FILLED.

Telephone 7943.

REIBER BROS., Prop'rs.

WALTER ST. JOHN JONES.
JAMES W. MONTGOMERY.
JOSEPH A. HAASS.

JONES, MONTGOMERY & CO.,

= Fire Insurance =

21 EAST THIRD STREET,

Third National Bank Building.   CINCINNATI, O.

TELEPHONE 698.

BURNET HOUSE
Shaving Parlor.

BEST WORKMANSHIP IN CITY.

JOHN SPENER, Proprietor.

A. KAPLUN,
Merchant Tailor,

New No. 339 Central Avenue,

(Grand Hotel Bldg.)   **CINCINNATI, O.**

Cleaning, Pressing, and Repairing done while you wait. Only First-Class Work made.

M. T. HOUGH,

.. IMPORTER OF ..

NOVELTIES IN FINE ❋ **MILLINERY,**

FANS, JEWELRY,
FANCY GOODS, Etc.

132 W. FOURTH ST.   CINCINNATI, O.
(NEW NUMBER, 106.)

LEIDING & CO.,

IMPORTERS AND DEALERS IN

CHINA, GLASS,
QUEENSWARE,
FANCY GOODS,
LAMPS,
SILVERWARE,
and CUTLERY,

409 Race Street,   CINCINNATI, O.

LATONIA SERIES

BAR SPOONS STRAINERS

BAR PITCHERS

LATONIA CUP, 1895.

MADE BY

THE DUHME COMPANY,

JEWELERS AND SILVERSMITHS,

Cor. West Fourth and Walnut Sts., Cincinnati, O.

Hollenden Hotel

FIRST-CLASS. CLEVELAND, OHIO.

American and European Plan. Under very liberal management. "Excellent Cuisine."

HOLLENDEN HOTEL CO.,
PROPRIETORS.

F. A. Brosius
MANAGER

CHAS. S. COWIE,

FASHIONABLE

Boot and Shoe Maker,

NEW No. 434 VINE STREET.   OLD No. 184 VINE STREET.
East Side, bet. Fourth and Fifth Streets.

Cincinnati, Ohio.

Agent for HANAN & SON and JOHNSTON & MURPHY, Fine Shoes.

J. H. KRIMPELMAN,

Hay, Grain, and Feed.

ALL KINDS COAL AND COKE.

Furniture Cars for Hire.

Packing and Shipping Done to Order.

Telephone 2124.

S. W. Cor. Fourth and Stone Streets,
CINCINNATI, O.

FRANK FOX,

Commission
- and -

Sale Stable

Telephone 942.

Horses kept by the Day, Week, or Month.

New Nos. 215 & 217 E. Fifth Street,
(Old No. 13 E. Fifth Street,)

CINCINNATI, O.

THE BEST LINE BETWEEN

Cincinnati and Chicago

The **ONLY LINE** operating the PULLMAN COMPARTMENT SLEEPING CAR between : : :

Cincinnati and Chicago

The **ONLY LINE** landing all Passengers . . . .

"Into the Heart of Chicago."

City Ticket Office, Chamber of Commerce,
Fourth and Vine.

DEPOT, Fifth and Baymiller.

D. G. EDWARDS, GENERAL PASSENGER AGENT,
Cincinnati, O.

Adolph M. Jordan,

Practical Optician

'TIS NATURAL TO SEE ..

But how few see well. Get your spectacles and eye-glasses from us, and have comfort. Get the Eclipse Eye-Glass. It Eclipses them all. Field and Race Glasses for the races.

45 East Fifth St.,

Corner Walnut,

OCULISTS' PRESCRIPTIONS FILLED PROMPTLY.

CINCINNATI, O.

JOHN P. EPPLY,
FUNERAL DIRECTOR AND EMBALMER,
Telephone 2189 & 669, Cincinnati, O.

Milton Keynes UK
Ingram Content Group UK Ltd.
UKHW010836010224
437095UK00013B/410